# Memories of Army Life
# and
# MPs of the 529th

*The Top Military Police Company*
*in the United States Army of the 1970s*

By R. Olin Jackson III
B.A., M.Ed.

Published by Whippoorwill Publications, LLC
Roswell, GA 30075

*Photography by Robert Walls, Jim Beardwood, Jack Williams, Lenny Addis,*
*Randy Duvall, Les Toon, R.O. Jackson*
*(and possibly others whose names have been lost over the past half century).*

<u>**Publisher's Note:**</u> *This work chronicles a portion of the history of the United States Army's 529th Military Police Company which originated in Europe in 1946. The descriptions of this unit, its men, their mission, notable accomplishments, and any unusual incidents are provided herewith – to the best of the author's memory after the passage of more than half a century of time – for the reader's interest and reference. Due to this direct association with the Armed Forces of the United States, the images and identifications of those appearing in the photographs and otherwise referenced within the military exigency of this book are public domain. Within the anecdotal and erstwhile humorous sections of this book, the names and identifying information of some of the participants have either been altered or omitted completely in order to protect the dignity of those involved. Within those sections, any presumed resemblance of the participants to any individuals – whether living or deceased today – is speculative and purely coincidental.*

ISBN: 979-8-9872286-6-1 (softback); 979-8-9872286-7-8 (hardback); 979-8-9872286-8-5 (eBook)

Library of Congress Control Number: 2023911396

Publisher's Cataloging-in-Publication Data
provided by Five Rainbows Cataloging Services
Names: Jackson III, Ralph Olin, 1951- author.
Title: Memories of army life and MPs of the 529th : the top military police company in the United States Army of the 1970s / Ralph Olin Jackson III.
Description: Roswell, GA : Whippoorwill Publications, 2023. | Includes index.
Identifiers: LCCN 2023911396 (print) | ISBN 979-8-9872286-6-1 (paperback) | ISBN 979-8-9872286-7-8 (hardcover) | ISBN 979-8-9872286-8-5 (ebook)
Subjects: LCSH: United States. Army—Military life. | North Atlantic Treaty Organization—Armed Forces—Biography. | United States. Army—Biography. | United States. Army—Foreign service—Germany (West) | Generals—United States. | United States—History, Military—20th century—Anecdotes. | BISAC: BIOGRAPHY & AUTOBIOGRAPHY / Military. | HISTORY / Modern / 20th Century / Cold War.
Classification: LCC U53.J33 J34 2023 (print) | LCC U53.J33 (ebook) | DDC 355.0092—dc23.

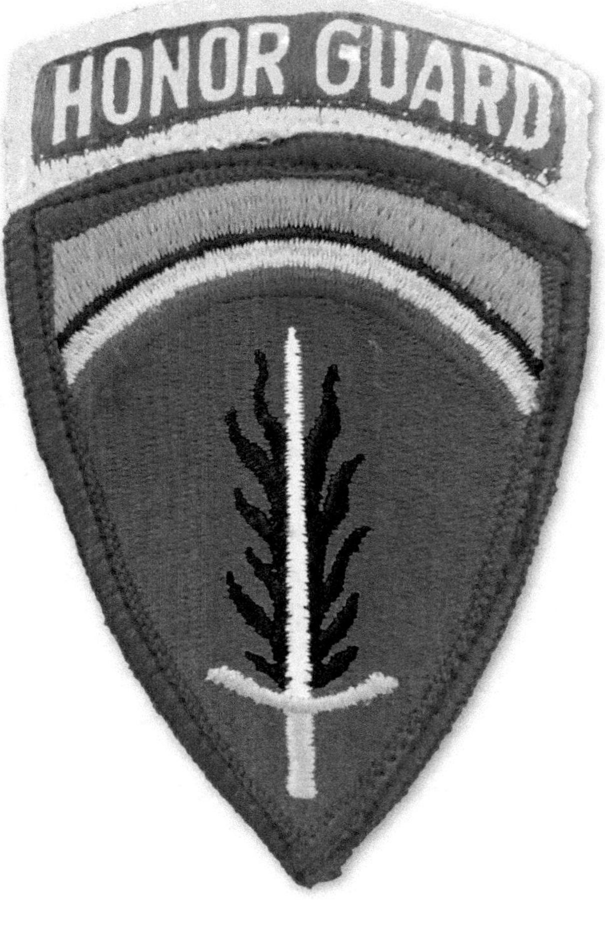
HONOR GUARD

# Contents

HEIDELBERG CASTLE - The ancient castle visible in this photo is an exceedingly historic landmark of Germany, intimately known by all those who served in the 529th M.P. Company. The castle ruins are among the most important Renaissance structures extant north of the Alps. The earliest castle structure on this site was built before 1214 and later expanded into two castles circa 1294. In 1537, a singular but exceedingly powerful lightning bolt amazingly destroyed the upper castle. The present castle structures had been expanded by 1650, before damage by later wars and fires diminished them. In 1764, yet another powerful lightning bolt caused a fire which destroyed some of the rebuilt sections.

THE OLD BRIDGE - The historic Karl Theodor Bridge, known by most as "the Old Bridge," is a traditional historic "arch" conveyance across the scenic Neckar River. It connects the ancient portion of Heidelberg (foreground) with the eastern portion of the Neuenheim district of the city on the opposite bank. The current bridge, built of Neckar sandstone, was commissioned by Elector Charles Theodor in 1788, and is the ninth-such structure built on this site. The center span was destroyed by the Nazis during World War II as a portion of their "scorched earth" policy during the final months of the war and was rebuilt at the war's conclusion.

# Foreword

The information and photographs on the pages which follow are not created or produced by, nor associated with, nor sanctioned by the Armed Forces of the United States. They are merely the observations, experiences, and recorded memories of a soldier in the 529th Military Police Company in Heidelberg, Germany, from April of 1972 to December of 1974.

Nevertheless, all of the details described herein actually occurred and are chronicled here for posterity. They are revealed from the perspective of one who was there.

The writer – R. Olin Jackson – volunteered for service in the United States Army in December of 1971. Following Basic Training and Advanced Individual Training (AIT), he was assigned to the 529th Military Police in April of 1972, where he served as a security guard on gates at Patton and Campbell Barracks in Heidelberg from April to September of 1972, including the period during which terrorists detonated two devastating improvised explosive devices (IEDs) within Campbell.

In October of 1972, "Spec-4 Jackson" was assigned to duty in the United States Army Europe's highly-sensitive USAREUR Command Building where he was a member of the security team for the Commander-in-Chief of the United States Army in Europe General Michael S. Davison, and his offices and staff therein. In addition to this duty, Spec-4 Jackson was also assigned to the USAREUR "Color Guard" detachment traveling throughout Europe in representation of the USAREUR Command.

The information on the following pages seeks to offer a glimpse of the lives of the soldiers of the 529th in the early 1970s who, in 1974, were rated and officially named as the top military police company in the United States Army worldwide. The author has done his best to include details and anecdotes involving all the men of the 529th with whom he served and for whom "memories" could be dredged up for this time-period.

Since the names, actual identities and photographs of those soldiers operational in an official U.S. military capacity fall generally into the realm of "public domain," they are freely used and provided herewith. However, the names, identities, and photographs of those soldiers in an 'off-duty' capacity from whom permissions for the use of their identities and photographs have not been forthcoming have either been shielded via pseudonyms, or they have been omitted entirely from this publication.

Grateful appreciation is herewith extended to Sgt. Robert "Wally" Walls, Spec-4 Les Toon, Spec-4 Lenny Addis, and Spec-4 Ed Meek for their assistance with the information and photographs necessary for this publication.

# Chapter 1

### ∽

# History of the 529ᵗʰ

If we trace it back to its original roots, the 529ᵗʰ Military Police (MP) Company, formerly of Heidelberg, Germany, was actually constituted on June 28, 1945, as the 153ʳᵈ Military Police Service Company, with service in New Delhi, India, commencing on July 13, 1945. On December 28, 1946, the 153rd was re-organized in Europe and re-designated as the 529ᵗʰ Military Police "Service" Company, with assignment to the European Command at Giessen, Germany. Finally, on June 22, 1951, the 529ᵗʰ Military Police "Service" Company was re-designated simply as the 529ᵗʰ Military Police Company and transferred to La Rochelle, France, where it remained until December of 1952, when it was transferred to the United States Army Europe (USAREUR) headquarters in Heidelberg, where it remained until 2013.

As such, though the 529ᵗʰ has roots in the approximate time-period as famed World War II General George S. Patton (who died tragically on December 21, 1945), the nearest it ever came to any direct association with the general was in the fact that the 529ᵗʰ was billeted for roughly 61 years in barracks in Heidelberg which had been named in honor and memory of the great general.

Gen. Patton, however, did have a direct connection with Heidelberg itself, in that following the automobile accident in which he was involved just outside

Mannheim which ultimately took his life, he was transported to and treated for several weeks at the U.S. Army's 130ᵗʰ Station Hospital in Heidelberg. Gen. Patton ultimately died in this facility, and his funeral was conducted nearby at Christuskirche (Christ Church), Zähringerstrasse 26, Heidelberg as well, only a mile or two from what came to be known as Patton Barracks.

Though its personal association with the great general was almost nonexistent, the 529ᵗʰ was, nevertheless, a storied unit in its own right. It came near to winning or won outright a number of prestigious awards for military merit over the years, such is the excellence demanded of the unit's men.

In 1973, competing against approximately 190+ U.S. Army military police units, the 529ᵗʰ was named "First Runner-Up" for the coveted *Brigadier General Jeremiah P. Holland Award* identifying the top military police company in the entire United States Army – worldwide.

In 2009, the 529ᵗʰ was recognized once again for its superiority, receiving the *Griffin Award* as the top military police Company in Europe. In 2012, the unit's final year to be headquartered in Heidelberg, it was "First Runner-Up" for the *Holland Award*, again as the top military police company in the Army worldwide. In 1974, the 529th won this award outright.

More importantly – these accolades notwithstanding – during the decade of the 1970s, the 529th in Heidelberg successfully safe-guarded the commander-in-chief (CINC) of the United States Army in Europe, the deputy-CINC, their administrative offices and staff in the USAREUR Command Building, the residences of the CINC and D-CINC, and much more, for all of the aforementioned 61 years that the unit was headquartered in Heidelberg. That, in itself, is an achievement of the highest regard.

During its period of residency in Heidelberg, the 529th was considered the sister-organization of the fabled "Old Guard" honor guard company in Washington, D.C. It required much the same excellence and quality of its troops, though it did not train in close-order drills with M-14 rifles to the same degree as did the Old Guard. The men of the 529th were more oriented toward protection and defense as garrison troops.

The 529th MPs also were not trained professionally to the degree of Army "Rangers" or "Special Forces," even though some of the officer and NCO leadership were Army Rangers. All the men of the 529th were, nevertheless, held to extremely high standards, and were officially designated as "Special Troops" by the Army.

In the periodic honor guard ceremonies for which the 529th is responsible, the troops wear the same dress-blue uniforms as do the Washington, D.C. "Old Guard," sporting the same M-14 ceremonial rifles. Each soldier in the Old Guard is required to be in superb physical condition, possess an unblemished military record and be between 5 feet, 10 inches and 6 feet, 4 inches tall for men or 5 feet, 8 inches and 6 feet, 2 inches tall for women, with a proportionate weight and build. The men of the Heidelberg 529th were held to equally high standards of appearance and excellence.

In addition to the qualifications described above, in order to qualify for inclusion in the 529th – particularly as regarded duty in the highly-sensitive USAREUR Command Building – those assigned to this duty were required to have Top-Secret security clearances and have demonstrated exceptional leadership capabilities, to be highly qualified in small arms usage, and preferably to have attended some measure of post-high school education.

In July of 2012, the 529th Military Police Company was permanently relocated from Heidelberg to Wiesbaden, Germany, as part of the USAREUR transformation, and assigned to the 709th Military Police Battalion and 18th MP Brigade headquartered in Grafenwohr, Germany.

In addition to its combat support mission today, the 529th in Wiesbaden provides 24/7 law enforcement in support of United States Army Group (USAG) in Wiesbaden and Italy, and continues its traditional ceremonial role as USAREUR's "Honor Guard." It has a number of other deployment obligations each year as well.

The stories, background and anecdotes of the 529th on the pages which follow all occurred while the unit was yet headquartered in historic Heidelberg. In the interest of sensitivity, the identities of selected individuals have been altered. The focus of this particular account of the 529th takes place in Heidelberg from 1972 to 1975, but includes some details from the Heidelberg years beyond the 1970s time-frame.

# Chapter 2

~

# Arrival in Heidelberg

In early April of 1972, following stints of Basic Training at Fort Knox, Kentucky, and Advanced Individual Training (AIT) at Fort Gordon, Georgia, I found myself first on a scheduled flight to New Jersey. From there, I changed flights to a jumbo jet filled almost entirely with G.I.s. We traveled eastward to Scotland before continuing on to Frankfurt, West Germany.

My ultimate European duty station destination was the United States Army in Europe (USAREUR) Headquarters Command in Heidelberg, West Germany. *(At that time, with the Cold War still very much a part of the political reality and the Soviet Union still intact, Germany was still divided into Communist "East Germany" and Allied-controlled "West Germany.")*

As the site of the U.S. Command Headquarters, Heidelberg was the largest U.S. installation in Europe at that time. The United States Army in Europe as well as the Army branch of NATO, were commanded by four-star Gen. Michael S. Davison.

As a young officer, Davison had served in World War II, where he was assigned to the 45th Infantry Division in North Africa. He remained with the division in Sicily and Italy, to include taking part in the Anzio Invasion. At the age of 26, he was chosen to command the 1st Battalion, 179th Infantry Division. Four months later he was promoted to lieutenant colonel, and he remained

commander of the battalion throughout the Italian campaign and the invasion of southern France. During his time with the 179th, he was wounded twice.

After the war, then-Colonel Davison earned a master's degree in Public Administration from Harvard University in 1951 (and that was back when Harvard was truly academically challenging). In 1958, he graduated from the U.S. military's National War College. In 1960, he was chosen to lead Combat Command A, 3rd Armored Division, where he was soon promoted to brigadier general and assigned as Chief of Staff of V Corps.

Davison was next promoted to lieutenant general in 1968, and appointed as Deputy Commander-in-Chief, United States Army – Pacific. In 1970, he assumed command of II Field Force Command, and was responsible for conducting the Cambodian Campaign in Southeast Asia.

In the USAREUR post, General Davison had some 220,000 troops under his command, one of which was me. The administrative offices for the sprawling USAREUR command were located at what was known as "Campbell Barracks," and the security therein was provided by the 529th Military Police Company headquartered in nearby Patton Barracks.

Though I never thought about it at the time, 1972 was only a short 27 years after the end of World War II. Looking back, it amazes me today, because World

3

During the height of World War II in Europe in 1944, Gen. Michael S. Davison was in the small French town of Meximieux, his unit tactically divided as the Allies chased retreating German army forces northward. When a German armored division turned to counter-attack its pursuers, then-Col. Davison and his men suddenly found themselves surrounded, out-manned and outgunned by the audacious Germans. The battle between the opposing forces raged for two days until the Germans eventually were forced to abandon their counter-offensive and continue their retreat northeastward. For his heroic actions at Meximieux, Col. Davison was awarded the "Silver Star," the third-highest combat military decoration in the U.S. Armed Forces. By the end of the war, he had been wounded twice, received the Bronze Star for gallantry in action and awarded numerous additional ribbons and commendations, including the coveted Combat Infantryman's Badge. Following many subsequent post-war assignments throughout the military establishment of the United States worldwide – including the Vietnam era – "General" Davison was, in 1971, named as the Commander in Chief of the United States Army in Europe with headquarters in Heidelberg, Germany, during a time of heightened tensions resulting from extremely murderous terrorist activities being conducted by the children of former Nazi personnel in Germany. He, in effect, had come "full-circle."

War II was such a momentous and historic event about which I learned from old black and white news-clip film footage of the war and its devastation upon Germany and the other Axis nations.

Upon my arrival at Rhein Mein Air Force Base in Frankfurt, Germany in the dead of night, I distinctly recall seeing some of the remaining detritus of war: things like an aged locomotive on a side-track in a rail yard with bullet holes stitched across it; and an occasional large masonry building here and there still etched with the devastations of artillery rounds, aerial bombs and rifle-fire.

Rhein Mein Air Force Base is only a memory today. It was once the largest American Air Force base in Europe, and prior to that, it had been a major air base of Nazi Germany's Luftwaffe before and during World War II. In 1999, however, it was closed permanently, after the conclusion of the Cold War after Pentagon planners decided it was no longer of any strategic use. Interestingly, I suspect the emerging conflicts in the Middle East and a resurgent Russia in later years caused some of those same planners to regret their lack of foresight in retaining control of the famed air base.

During World War II, the Battle of Frankfurt was a four-day struggle for control of the German city which had been a Nazi Army stronghold. The U.S. 5th Mechanized Infantry Division conducted the main attack while the U.S. 6th Armored Division provided support.

The 5th Infantry crossed the Rhine on 22 March and quickly established a bridgehead. By 23 March, the 5th had expanded its bridgehead five miles east, putting the division only 14 miles southwest of Frankfurt. Armored Task Forces pushed northward from the bridgehead towards Trebur and Gustaysburg, and to the East towards Darmstadt.

On 25 March, the Wehrmacht (Nazi armed forces) commander of the Darmstadt garrison surrendered and the city of Darmstadt was relinquished to the U.S. 6th Armored and 5th Infantry Divisions. By 26 March, the 5th reached the southern outskirts of the city of Frankfurt and captured Rhein Mein airbase.

*(Interestingly, in 1955 when West Germany was allowed by the occupying forces to rebuild its military, the new German armed forces organization was called the "Bundeswehr," not the Wehrmacht. While it originally unavoidably employed many former Nazi troops, it was not considered a successor to the Wehrmacht and avoided any such association.)*

Meanwhile, the U.S. 6th Armored linked up with the 5th and pushed through the southern outskirts of Frankfurt (Sachsenhausen) to the river Main. There, units of the 5th discovered to their delight a mostly intact Wilhelmsbruecke Bridge *(known today as the Friedensbruecke Bridge)*. German engineers had rigged explosives and desperately attempted to destroy the bridge in a last-ditch effort to slow the advance of US Forces on 25 March, but that effort failed miserably.

Supported by U.S. tank artillery, the troops of the 5th crossed the Wilhelmsbruecke under heavy fire on 27 March and entered the northern part of Frankfurt. The two divisions then fought the Germans in fierce house-to-house combat, slowly pushing through the city to the north and to the east. For these and other reasons, the city of Frankfurt still bore many scars of war right up until the early 1970s.

After departing Rhein Mein Air Base in the early morning hours of a somewhat warm April day in 1972, I was (along with several other enlistees) bussed approximately 55 miles to the

The final stage of World War II in the European Theatre commenced with the Western Allied invasion of Germany and the crossing of the Rhine River in March of 1945. Gen. George Patton knew his entrance into German-occupied territory was of monumental historical importance. His remarkable achievements in the World War II arena remain as some of the greatest in the history of the United States, but he was ultimately rejected and dismissed to a paper army status in the autumn of 1945, when his popularity and public statements threatened the rising political career of Gen. Dwight Eisenhower. Patton (r) is pictured in Germany with Eisenhower (c) and Gen. Omar Bradley (l) who replaced him in rank and authority in 1945. (U.S. Army staff photo)

south to the very picturesque and historic town of Heidelberg on the Neckar River. It included a historic old-town section, a massive ancient partially-destroyed castle, and a very storied past.

As we arrived in the town, our bus pulled through the front gate of an installation we noticed was emblazoned with the name "Patton Barracks," which I found interesting. I didn't know it at the time, but the famed U.S. Army general's last command was just north of Frankfurt, and he in fact had died at the U.S. Army's 130th Station Hospital in Heidelberg.

# Chapter 3

# Famed Gen. George S. Patton in Heidelberg

By the end of April, 1945, the war in Europe was winding down. Germans were surrendering en masse to American and British forces to avoid being taken by the dreaded Russian battalions. Gen. George S. Patton and his famed Third Army located in southwestern Germany were advancing northeastward. When Patton reached the Rhine River near the ancient town of Trier, he knew from his long studies of history that he was traveling on the same roads that Julius Caesar and his legions once had trod 2,000 or more years earlier in their campaigns against Gall, and it delighted him.

Patton had been instructed by his superiors not to cross the Rhine nor to attempt to take the city of Trier. The determined and crafty general, however, conquered the city anyway after a difficult engagement with remaining Nazi troops. When later reprimanded by Supreme Allied Commander Dwight Eisenhower, Patton quickly characteristically retorted *"Well what do you want me to do? Give it back?"*

As the last cities and strongholds were conquered, the old warhorse began receding gradually into depression. He was a battle-horse and lived for warfare. *"God help me I do love it,"* he once stated.

Moreover, Patton found the submissiveness of his superiors to Russia to

A World War II publicity print of Patton prior to receiving his fourth star.

be appalling, sensing the terrible mistake they were making. He felt certain that one day in the near future – without a doubt – America would be forced to wage war against the Russians, and that it was absolutely foolish to remove American troops and weapons and abdicate America's overwhelming power in Europe when the U.S. had the opportunity at hand to conquer Russia and be done with it.

Gen. Dwight Eisenhower, however, looked at the picture from a totally different perspective. He was well aware that America and its allies were weary of war and wanted the conflict brought to a quick conclusion. Though he had not made it publicly known, Eisenhower also had political aspirations for the White House, and any miss-step in quickly ending the war could negatively impact his budding political career.

Patton, on the other hand, stated publicly that all the geo-political talk about creating an international organization known as "the United Nations" to keep peace in the world essentially was *"pissing in the wind." "As long as man is man,"* he said, *"there will be war, and the only way to avoid trouble is to have the best army and navy – which we now have. . . . and the sooner we fight the Russians, the better."*

Patton's comments in this regard enraged Eisenhower, who not only wanted the war concluded, but a total "de-Nazification" of Europe as well. He abhorred anything regarding a negative perspective of Russia, believing that to simply be counter-productive to his goals.

Regarding Eisenhower's "de-Nazification" orders, Patton, again, was of a different opinion. He felt that the overwhelming purge of Nazis from Germany was leaving it weakened even more than the inflictions which had already been imposed by the Allies. He feared the trajectory of the Russians in Europe much more than the Nazis at that point. He felt the Nazi purging was causing the infrastructure of Germany to fall into the hands of un-trained, incapable administrators and underlings in the only nation that could serve as a present and future bulwark across Eastern Europe against the ever-growing threat of communist Russia.

In his expression of these sentiments, however, Patton made a huge

Pvt. Horace Woodring examines the damaged Cadillac limousine in which he was driving Gen. Patton just outside Mannheim, Germany, at the time of the fatal accident which resulted in the general's death. He stated at the time that the splotches upon his jacket were from the general's blood.

miss-step, handing Eisenhower an opportunity to at least partially rid himself of the nettlesome general. Patton callously publicly stated that he personally felt no one – Nazi or otherwise – should be removed from a job or have property confiscated *"without the successful proof of guilt before a court of law,"* adding that after all, *"It is no more possible for a man to be a civil servant in Germany and not have paid lip service to Nazism than it is for a man to be a postmaster in America and not have paid lip service to the Democratic or Republican Party. . ."*

Those simple words which had been uttered quite innocently nevertheless lit a firestorm of outrage, not the least of which came from Eisenhower. Though history has borne out Patton's statements as exceptionally pragmatic and ultimately very accurate, that did nothing at the time to save him from a high-level group of government officials

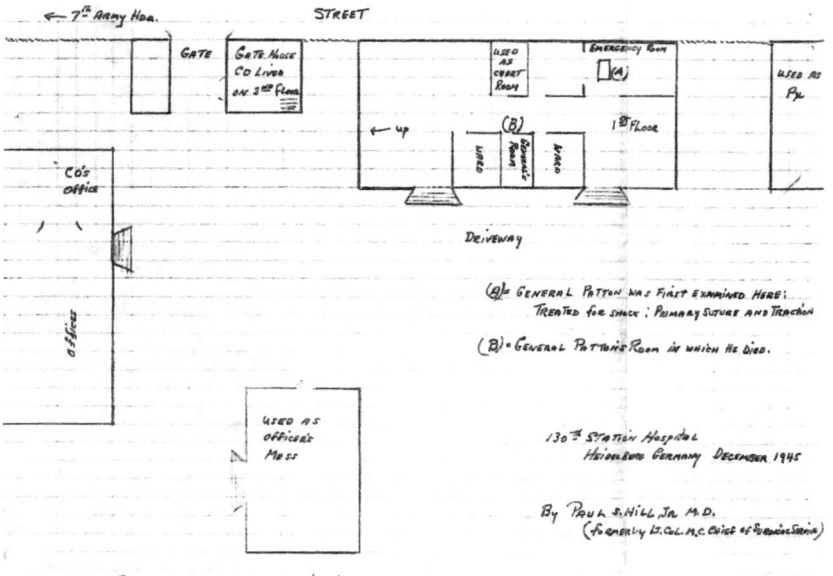

A diagram drawn by Dr. (formerly Lt. Col.) Paul Hill, Jr., former chief of Surgical Services at the 130th Station Hospital in Heidelberg. This sketch clearly shows the room in which Gen. Patton was housed and in which he died in December of 1945. As is obvious from the diagram, the hospital offered very limited treatment facilities at that time.

Gen. George S. Patton spent the final weeks of his life at this small hospital in Heidelberg. Photographed here circa 1960, the 130th Station Hospital memorialized the room in which the great general died right up until 2013, after which all U.S. troops were relocated out of Heidelberg and all properties returned to the ownership of the German government.

– including Eisenhower – who were determined to destroy him.

When this occurred, Patton was the military governor of Germany, ensconced in quarters in Bavaria. In a retort to Eisenhower's repudiation of his comments, Patton made known that he was certain Eisenhower was positioning himself for a political career following the culmination of the war, and that he was unnecessarily sacrificing men and might in his obsessive pacification of the Russians in order to quickly end the war and begin that career.

Following a public rebuke, he (Patton) threatened to resign from the military and expose what he felt was a great amount of callous activity which had been conducted by Eisenhower and others at the expense of American lives. As elements transpired, this proved to be an even worse mistake on Patton's part.

In late September, 1945, in a further repudiation of his statements, Eisenhower took the harshest step yet imposed against his most elite general. He

8

A modern (2023) view of the front entrance of the former facilities of the 130th Station Hospital in Heidelberg. The hospital's front gate is visible lower right corner. The earlier portion of the original hospital building in which Gen. Patton was treated and died is visible center-left. (Photo courtesy of U.S. Government)

A 2023 view from inside the hospital grounds looking toward the front entrance of the former 130th Station Hospital. Also pictured are several of the original buildings dating from Patton's day and earlier in the 1930s when the property was controlled by Nazi Germany. (Photo courtesy of U.S. Government)

According to a diagram drawn by Dr. (formerly Lt. Col.) Paul Hill, Chief of Surgical Services at 130th Station Hospital in Heidelberg, the small peaked building in the top left corner of this photo beside the front gate entrance into the hospital facilities was the living quarters of the commanding officer of the hospital in 1945. The structure with the doubled-peaked dormer fronts beside it was the building in which Gen. Patton was hospitalized. The general was in a lower-level room in the front centered between the two dormers. This aerial view was photographed in 2023 after the former 130th Station Hospital facility had been abandoned by the U.S. military. (Photo courtesy of U.S. Government)

A modern view (2023) of Christ Church in Heidelberg where the 1945 funeral for Gen. George S. Patton was conducted.

permanently removed Patton – the most famous and winningest general of World War II and one of the most effective leaders in American history – from command of his beloved Third Army.

Making the matter even worse, on a rainy day in October of 1945, Eisenhower reassigned Patton as commander of the Fifteenth Army – essentially a paper affair which in actuality was a small task force charged with writing the history of the U.S. Army's actions in Europe. Patton considered this the ultimate slap in the face, and, in fact, a most shameful demotion.

Patton's new headquarters was the town of Bad Nauheim, a small town approximately 17 miles north of Frankfurt.

The honor guard escort for General Patton's body during his funeral in December of 1945.

(It, interestingly, is the town in which Adolf Hitler's famous command post – "Adlerhorst" – was located. It also is the site of the home in which famed musical performer Elvis Presley would live a few years later in 1958 during his service in the U.S. Army.)

With this new assignment, Patton couldn't have been more depressed. The war was quickly coming to a conclusion and abject boredom was setting in. Rambling around his Bad Nauheim quarters, he also learns that his previous night's dinner guest and long-time friend Maj. Gen. Geoffrey Keyes, commander of the 7th Army, has been recalled to his quarters on urgent business.

Keyes is one of the general's few remaining close friends in Europe, and a favored armored commander upon whom Patton had greatly depended during the Sicilian Campaign. To relieve some of the monotony of his circumstances and his disappointment at Keye's departure, Patton decided he would go pheasant hunting southward in the vicinity of Mannheim.

On Sunday, December 9, 1945, Patton – with his new driver PFC Horace Woodring and his friend Gen. Hap Gay – set out for the hunt. Reaching the outskirts of Mannheim – which had been much-destroyed in the war – he was gazing at all the detritus of the battles when a huge Army deuce-and-a-half truck suddenly and inexplicably veered directly into the path of Patton's olive-drab Cadillac limousine. PFC Woodring made his best attempt to avoid the heavy truck, but all his efforts were in vain.

The resulting heavy crash did not injure Gay nor Woodring, but Patton, in contrast, was seriously injured. His nose was smashed and broken and his scalp was completely peeled back from his forehead to the crown of his head. Worse than that, however, the general realized the impact of his head with the

11

divider between the front and rear seats in the limousine had broken his neck, and he was completely paralyzed from his neck to his toes.

The general was quickly transported to the nearby 130th Station Hospital in Heidelberg, but despite the importance of the medical emergency, no medical staff-members were waiting to rush Patton into surgery, nor were there any specialists on hand whatsoever. The hospital, admittedly, was a tiny facility at that time, and the medical staff therefore was extremely limited.

Experts, nevertheless were summoned as soon as possible, and they worked on him feverishly for several weeks in an attempt to save him. Amazingly, after weeks of treatment it was believed Patton was well enough to be transported home to America, but before this could take place, he suffered a pulmonary embolism which proved fatal, and died on December 20, 1945.

Following a funeral at Christ Church in Heidelberg, Patton's body was transported westward by train to the American cemetery in Luxembourg where he was buried. During the "Battle of the Bulge" at which Patton had gained national fame, he ironically had been headquartered in this same town.

Equally ironic, had he not succumbed to his penchant for controversial public comments, Patton might have been the first commander of the United States Army in Europe headquartered in Heidelberg. As such, it seems

*During the "Battle of the Bulge" at which Patton had gained national fame, he ironically had been headquartered in this same town.*

only fitting that the barracks in that town – which later housed a portion of the American contingent as well as the 529th Military Police Company – be named for Patton.

Has history proven that much of what Patton proclaimed and foretold in 1945 has come true? In point of fact, it has.

The onset of the Cold War between the United States and the Soviet Union against the backdrop of a divided Europe was precisely the circumstances Patton had predicted and dreaded. The ultimate ascension of Dwight Eisenhower to the White House was correctly foretold as well, as was the fact that the days of an isolationist United States protected by the expanses of the Atlantic and Pacific Oceans would soon come to a close with the advance of technology.

*"They now say that we've got 3,000 miles of ocean to protect America,"* he stated in 1945, *"but 20 years from now, this 3,000 miles of ocean will be just like a good spit. This is a very serious thing, and many people don't visualize this very grave danger* (with Russia and terrorist nations)." His words proved to be ominously prophetic.

For many years, the room in which Patton was treated at the 130th Station Hospital was maintained as a memorial to the great but controversial general. Since the site was returned to German control in 2013, the status and destiny of his room and this hospital are now unknown.

## Chapter 4

~

# 1970s Life at Patton and Campbell Barracks

I remember that it was so foggy on that April morning of my arrival in 1972, that I was unable to see more than a few feet in front of me as I exited the bus which had transported us from Rhein-Mein Air Base in Frankfurt to Heidelberg. To this day I still don't know how that bus driver was able to maneuver that vehicle, because that fog truly was "pea-soup."

As the bus pulled away, we were left standing on a street corner in Patton Barracks. There was a military policeman manning the front gate, and, noticing our confusion, he directed us to the billeting office for new troops in a large, imposing structure which formerly had been used to house Nazi troops. This was to become my home for the next year or so until I was able to move "off-post" to more exciting accommodations in downtown in Heidelberg.

I also remember the barracks that morning as being cold, massive and forbidding. This building – one of numerous in this compound once collectively identified as "Grenadier Kaserne" by the Nazis – had clearly been used by armed forces long before it was taken over by American troops in 1946. I would later learn that the 110th Infantry Division of Nazi Germany had been housed in this three-story barracks building from the early 1900s to the mid-1940s, by which

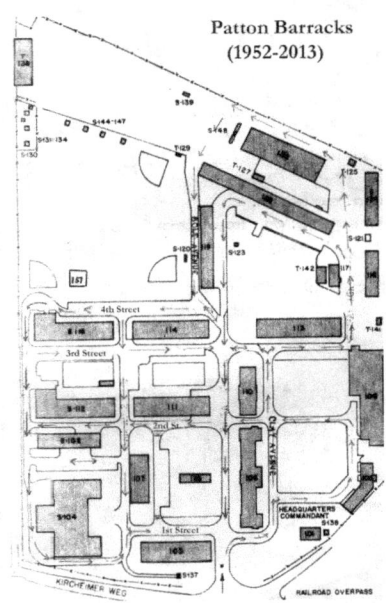

Patton Barracks
(1952-2013)

A diagram of Patton Barracks as it appeared from 1952 to 2013.

The entrance to Patton Barracks from the front street (Kircheimer Weg). The barracks housing the 529th M.P. Company are out of sight on the left.

13

Photographed in 1973, this view from inside Patton Barracks looks toward the street (Kircheimer Weg) in front of Patton. The little refreshments/food stand known for decades as "Pops" is visible in the background. As far as is known, Gen. George S. Patton never set foot inside his namesake barracks in Heidelberg.

Also photographed in 1973, this view of Building 103 at Patton Barracks looks toward Flaming Sword Service Club. (Photo by Bob Walls. Reprinted with Permission.)

Photographed in 2015, Building 103 at Patton Barracks has undergone extensive renovation for continued future use. All the old trappings which once identified it as the home of the 529th and 536th MP Companies however, have disappeared. (Photo by Bob Walls)

time, the bulk of the division had been decimated on the Eastern Front and in North Africa.

Prior to use by the 110th, this building had housed the personnel overseeing one of Germany's World War I prisoner-of-war camps on this site. I remember that all up and down the long hallways of

Building 103 in which I was housed, ancient rifle racks had been built into the walls to hold the heavy German Mauser rifles which once had been a staple of Nazi Germany's infantry.

There were in fact numerous massive

Each morning, prior to proceeding to their various security details, the MPs of the 529th were first required to stand for a stiff inspection at "Guard Mount." This photo was taken in 1973, at the unit's temporary billets near the Patton NCO Club which were occupied while Building 103 was undergoing a renovation. (Photo by Bob Walls)

Sgt. Bob Walls at the helm as desk sergeant at the Patton gate. With a quick smile and easy-going personality, he nevertheless was all business at the gates.

SFC Leece closely examines the uniforms at Guard Mount to make certain everything conforms to regulation and beyond. The individual with the top uniform each day was awarded the day off. (Photo by Bob Walls)

masonry buildings in this military compound now called "Patton Barracks." Contrary to the style of American military installation construction, the Germans didn't build hammer-and-nail wooden structures, but instead built everything with steel-reinforced masonry materials and heavy concrete designed to

Built by the German Army circa 1911, this impoundment, known at this time as Grenadier Kaserne, exists where Patton Barracks later existed in Heidelberg. The building which later housed the 529th and 536 MP Companies from 1952 to 2013 at this site stands upper left-rear. At the time of this photo circa 1917, a compound (foreground) had been constructed as a prisoner-of-war stockade where captured British, French and American Army personnel were incarcerated during World War I.

A view of the interior quadrangle of Patton Barracks from Building 103, with the church in the foreground. This area was originally a World War I prisoner-of-war stockade in which French, English and American soldiers were incarcerated. (Photo by Bob Walls. Reprinted with permission.)

withstand bomb blasts and last for centuries. Many of those heavily-reinforced buildings, constructed in the early 1900s, are still standing today, and continue to be used throughout Germany.

The Nazi 110th Infantry Division which had once been billeted in this

Sgt. (1st Sergeant later in his career) Francis Carter Scruggs Withers of Charlottesville, Virginia, was a popular non-commissioned officer among the enlisted men in the 529th. He is pictured (circa 1972) at the front of the 529th MP barracks "holding court" as he often did. To Withers' rear just beyond the tall shrubs is the area once enclosed as a prisoner-of-war stockade during World War I.

16

The bar in the lower level of Building 103, the 529th M.P. Company barracks. Just outside this bar, the 529th also had a game room with "fooseball," table-tennis (ping-pong), and a regulation billiards table to name some of the entertainment. (Photo by Bob Walls)

A view of the old 529th M.P. billets in Building 103 at Patton Barracks from the front street (Kircheimer Weg), photographed 1973. From 1952 through 2012, this structure was occupied almost continuously (almost three-quarters of a century) by the MPs of the 529th. (Photo by Bob Walls)

Looking down from the second story south end window of the 529th barracks, this photo, taken in 1972, provides a view of the enlisted men's Flaming Sword Service Club.

structure was an elite unit which fought through some of the most devastating and major battles of the First World War, as well as on the Russian Front in 1941, and later, as elements of famed Nazi General Erwin Rommel's renowned Afrika Korps in North Africa in 1943. As a result of the heavy fighting they were forced to endure, they also suffered correspondingly heavy casualties.

Photographed in 2015, the former "Flaming Sword Service Club" had been abandoned for three years. The old Patton PX is visible left. (Photo by Bob Walls)

This "second" Front or "east" Gate at Campbell occasionally was not operational (open) during the day, and never at night or weekends. (Photo by Bob Walls)

The front or "east" entrance of Campbell Barracks as viewed from Romerstrasse on what appears to be a weekend. The main MP operations desk at Campbell existed to the right (not pictured). The front entrance was open and secured by the 529th MPs 24 hours a day, seven days a week, 365 days a year.

This "walk-in" gate on the south side of Campbell also occasionally was not operational (open) during the day, and never at night or weekends. (Photo by Bob Walls)

SSG Ted Lawrence rides desk sergeant duty at the Campbell Barracks MP Center. From this office the desk sergeant monitored the MP Patrol Cruisers, Jeeps, the five gates surrounding Campbell Barracks, the Command Building, Patton Barracks and more, all tied together with various means of communication. (Photo by Bob Walls)

The north gate (Gate 2) at Campbell Barracks. This gate was closed during the evening hours and on weekends. All the gates had radio communications with the Operations Desk at Gate One. (Photo by Bob Walls)

Nazi troops assigned to the 110th Infantry in Heidelberg are pictured circa 1939. They were photographed at Building 13 of what later became Campbell Barracks in Heidelberg. The clean pressed uniforms and highly-polished boots belie the later harsh duty these troops would endure on the Eastern Front against Russian troops and in North Africa against British and American troops. Their ranks eventually were so decimated by the horrors of war that the 110th was disbanded altogether.

Pictured is a modern view of Building 13 at what once was known as Campbell Barracks (decommissioned in 2013) at the once-sprawling U.S. Army complex in Heidelberg, Germany. Prior to use by American troops, this was a Nazi Army installation and the home of the Nazi 110th Infantry. Today, much of it has been demolished.

A view of the parade field and front entrance building of what later became Campbell Barracks by occupying American troops. In the 1930s and up to circa 1943, the site pictured here was the home of the German Wehrmacht's 110th Infantry training installation in Heidelberg, Germany. A group – which appears to be company-size – of the 110th stands for inspection in 1942 in this photo.

Photographed from roughly the same spot as the photo above with Nazi troops, this more modern view obviously shows what once was the USAREUR Headquarters at Campbell Barracks shortly after being abandoned by American troops in 2012. This property has been returned to the ownership of the German government.

The Kircheim Weg Grenadier Kaserne (later Patton Barracks) was not large enough to accommodate the entire 110th German Infantry Division, so a new installation (later renamed "Campbell Barracks" by conquering U.S. troops) was built in 1937 approximately one mile away (as the crow flies) at what then was the outskirts of Heidelberg near the tiny community of Rohrbach. When completed, it and the Kircheim Weg facility were used collectively to house the 110th, and were therefore identified collectively by the Germans as "Grenadier Kaserne."

The regiment's headquarters, its 1st Battalion, and its two regimental support companies were located at the Romerstrasse facility (Campbell Barracks). The regiment's 3rd Battalion was stationed at what later became Patton Barracks (the Kircheim Weg facility).

Life at Patton for the men of the 529th definitely had its advantages and disadvantages. At some point in the 1960s, much of the lower level of the 529th's billets had been converted into a large game room. There was a billiards table, "fooseball" tables, table tennis, and a number of other diversions. The lower level also included a small bar and lounge.

This in-house pub had its own full-time bar-keeper who maintained a steady supply of beverages for thirsty soldiers. Since his entire duty revolved around management of this pub, the bar-keeper's job was an envied assignment by some of the men of the 529th.

Sadly, just as with most everything else, time eventually alters even the most durable of circumstances. Both Patton Barracks and Campbell Barracks were decommissioned by the American military in 2012, and returned to the control of the German government. The 529th Military Police Company – the

Members of Nazi Wehrmacht's 110th Infantry were photographed in 1942 during happier times. This doorway is located on the rear side of the front (Main) building at the entrance to the Nazi complex on Romerstrasse in Heidelberg, Germany, and still exists today. When the city was overtaken by U.S. Forces in 1945, the structure in this photo became part of the complex known until 2013 as Campbell Barracks. In the 1970s, the interior of this building just beyond the door was a public gifts shop.

pride of the United States Army in Europe – packed up everything and moved approximately 50 miles to the north (roughly 15 miles west of Frankfurt) to Wiesbaden where the company still exists as of this writing in 2023.

Today, what once was the sprawling U.S. Army Headquarters – Europe (Campbell and Patton Barracks) has simply ceased to exist, and portions of both complexes have been demolished and leveled for new development.

Campbell was just a portion of the infrastructure for which the 529th Military Police Company – established in 1952 – was charged with protecting. It

A more recent photo of the rear gate of the Romerstrasse facility (later Campbell Barracks) photographed circa 1974. The brick building in this photo also appears in the 1941 photo of German troops at this site.

Members of the Nazi 110th Infantry were photographed in 1941 during target practice in the vicinity of what later became the back (rear) gate into what was later renamed "Campbell Barracks" by the American troops when the U.S. Army took command of Heidelberg in 1945. The same structure in the right-rear area of this photo also appears in the adjacent photo of the more modern rear gate of Campbell Barracks.

(Campbell) had five entrances/exits, all of which were manned by "gate-guards" from the 529th. During the evening hours, all the gates were closed except the Main front Gate. On weekends, with much of the staff vacated, only the Main Gate again remained open and manned by the 529th.

Campbell Barracks was a somewhat large facility as military installations in Europe are concerned – and rightfully so – since it included the headquarters offices and management staff for all the other U.S. Army installations in Europe. It also had more general-grade officers per square foot than any other U.S. facility in Europe. The men of the 529th Military Police Company, therefore, were drilled in rendering the utmost respect, service, and courtesy to all officers and NCOs.

When the men of the 529th did encounter a problem with the officer-staff or anything else, a solution was immediately at hand. His name was Col. Charles Shay. As the Patton Post Commandant, he considered the 529th to be "his own." Few indeed were the individuals which he would allow to disabuse the 529th, but he also demanded excellence and quality from the Deuce-Nine.

Even though both Campbell and Patton Barracks were decommissioned and abandoned by U.S. Military forces in 2013, and even though the City of Heidelberg wished to redevelop this property, many of the historic German-built structures at these two sites have been retained as of this writing. Most of what has been dismantled and demolished was built on a much less massive basis by U.S. forces from the late 1940s through the 1980s. So for those GIs formerly assigned to either Patton or Campbell, much of what existed in your time there still exists today.

In the 1970s, the Operations Center of the 529th Military Police at Campbell Barracks was what was known as "the Information Center" at the front gate. Every week-day, upwards of ten MPs (but sometimes as few as six, depending upon the number of gates opened to traffic) and a desk sergeant were on duty there in 12-hour shifts. Out of the five gates, those that were open each had a guard – one hour "on" and one hour "off." Those MPs on their "off" hour took their break in the rear "break room" at the MP Operations Center, awaiting their next "turn" on the gates.

Any gates which were open to traffic at either Patton or Campbell Barracks were manned by the MPs of the 529th around the clock. No open gate was ever left unattended.

The MPs working these gates worked three daytime shifts, then three evening shifts, then had three days "off" in consecutive order. This gate-guard duty rotated through all the men of the 529th who were not assigned to the Command Building, the War Room, the CINC's residence, or the U.S. Army airfield in Heidelberg. Occasionally, we worked five days on and four days off.

During my two and three-quarter years in the 529th, one of the additional "fixtures" at the Visitor Center was a wizened and irritable old German civilian who had been hired by the U.S. command to "run interference" with any Germans or foreign nationals who could not speak English and who had nevertheless presented themselves at the Visitor Center for entry into Campbell. His name was Hans Mueller.

I'm certain Hans has gone on to his

*The MPs working these gates worked three daytime shifts, then three evening shifts, then had three days "off" in consecutive order.*

"Greater Reward" by now, because he had to have been in his 50s or 60s when I was there in the 1970s. When he answered the landline telephone at the Operations Center stating "Mee-lee-teery Police!" one could almost imagine him in a Nazi German Wehrmacht uniform barking orders at underlings (which quite possibly had actually been the case in the 1940s).

Hans also was a chain-smoker, and I suspect that due to his employment by the U.S. military, he possibly had access to the PX and American cigarettes which he seemed to always have in abundance. With the air filled with his trademark tobacco smoke, he entertained no arguments from any non-American entities. Among them, his word was law, and he could be brutal too, sometimes becoming literally apoplectic in his anger.

As explained earlier, at the end of World War II, Gen. George S. Patton had instructed American forces in Germany to employ many men who had actually previously been Nazi troops – some in very high positions. He did this because he knew that virtually everyone in Germany had at least been a member of the Nazi Party and it would be impossible to find workers to jump-start the German economy who had not had at least a passing former allegiance to the Third Reich.

So, as repugnant as it was, Nazis had to be re-employed to re-start basic infrastructure of the devastated German economy such as the electrical systems, water and sewage treatment, and many other basic necessities of life.

# Chapter 5

# Amazing "Esprit de Corps"

Perhaps the most captivating aspect of the 529th Military Police Company – and one of the reasons for its designation as "the Army's finest" – was its amazing esprit de corps at a time when the United States Army was at its lowest ebb reputation-wise. I mean, let's face it, in the 1970s, the Army suffered from a tremendous image problem with the unfortunate circumstances in the Vietnam Conflict, the poor leadership in the White House, and much more.

I think it's more than fair to say that the G.I.s and enlistees of that day did not enjoy anywhere near the respect and admiration directed toward today's Army. Respect and admiration for the Army of the 1970s wasn't even a consideration. To the contrary, the military – particularly the United States Army – was almost universally reviled, abused, scorned and ridiculed if one admitted the truth – and this affected troop morale tremendously.

There were, however, units in the 1970s which nevertheless practiced and maintained a strong esprit de corps despite this poor image, and the 529th Military Police Company in Heidelberg was one of the brightest. When the Army needed a "pick-me-up," the "Deuce-Nine" shined liked no other, becoming the goodwill and image ambassadors not only of the Army, but of our nation in general. Those officers and NCOs who had committed their lives to a career in the military and who were exposed to the excellence of the 529th Military

Police Company demonstrated their appreciation for this quality time and time again.

Aside from 529th's responsibilities in the decade of the 1970s as security specialists and protective agents of the commander-in-chief of the United States Army in Europe and his headquarters staff, the unit was also an "honor guard" company, charged with a duty to "shine" for the military, and "shine" it did.

Both then and still today, the Deuce-Nine made one proud to be an American. The men and the might of the 529th just seethed pride, dignity and respect, and this was at least part of the reason they were selected as the *"Top Military Police Company in the United States Army"* in 1974.

Contingents of the 529th regularly conducted honor guard ceremonies throughout Europe using the old wooden-stocked M-14 rifles just like the "Old Guard" in Washington, D.C., and they were decked out in their distinctive eye-catching "dress-blue" uniforms in march-formation too. When this unit moved to a cadence at a military ceremony, heads turned, and for good reason.

The Deuce-Niners were precision instruments on the parade field. If they weren't meticulous in appearance and presentation when they marched in formation, they were required to endure hours of practice until they were. To the man, their training – both as security specialists and as disciplined visible goodwill ambassadors – was serious business. If they didn't take their job seriously, they didn't last very long in the Deuce-Nine.

Part of the mystique of the 529th M.P. Company over the years in Heidelberg included the unbelievably-impressive uniforms which the Deuce-Niners sported both in their security details and in the ceremonies in which they performed. How did they get those uniforms to look so sharp?

Deuce-Niners for several generations called this "getting strack." When someone in their midst had a really sharp uniform and boots, that individual would inevitably draw the comment: *"He's really 'strack.'"*

To this day I don't know the origin of the word *"strack."* It certainly isn't a standard term in the lexicon of American language. Someone back in the mists of time at the 529th undoubtedly just "created" the term, and it stuck.

So what did one actually "do" to become "strack?" Well, it involved hours and hours of starching and ironing knife-edged creases in the sleeves, shirt pockets, and pants of khaki and fatigue uniforms; polishing every single item of brass on a uniform to a brilliant sparkling finish; and spit-shining boots and Class-A shoes until one could see one's face in the toes and heels of every set of foot-ware.

All the "brass" on a uniform had to be meticulously polished until it sparkled like real gold. That included belt

*In order to get that brass to really shine, one had to first remove every microcosm of that stubborn lacquer.*

buckles, collar brass, marksmanship badges, hat brass and more, for starters. Anyone in the USAREUR "Color Guard" had still more brass to shine.

The method used to shine all this brass was unique as well. One began by buying or acquiring a simple newspaper. Any old newspaper would do. One also had to have a good supply of the ever-faithful *Brasso* polishing crème.

One next sat down on a firm table with a newspaper – several folds thick – spread upon the table-top with a liberal amount of *Brasso* splotched out on the paper. One then began rubbing the brass in the *Brasso* on the paper, back and forth, back and forth. Rubbing and polishing. Rubbing and polishing. Then working on the cracks and crevices in the brass with a polishing cloth. Hours of work.

"New" brass was the most difficult too. I don't know how it is today, but manufacturers back in the 1970s covered all new military insignia with a coating of lacquer to inhibit tarnishing. In order to get that brass to really shine, one had to first remove every microcosm of that stubborn lacquer. Only then would the metal shine to a lustrous finish.

With other items on the uniform such as the marksmanship qualification badges, after one had spent several hours polishing those with the *Brasso* on the newspaper, most of the ridges and definition on the front surface of the badges would be worn away, and one eventually would be left with a completely-smooth face which glimmered, sparkled, and

This promotional photograph was taken of members of the 529th Military Police Company in 1974, and subsequently was used in conjunction with U.S. Army recruiting posters. It demonstrates the various uniforms worn by the 529th in its many functions and responsibilities in Europe. Pictured standing (L-R) ground level are: Spec-4 Daniel Norman; Spec-4 Jean Claude Banks; unknown; and Spec-4 R.O. Jackson. Second level (L-R) are: Spec-4 Lenny Addis; Spec-4 Donald Hansen. Third level: unknown. Fourth level (L-R) are: SSG Patrick Mackay; Spec-4 Terrell Brocksmith; and Spec-4 Jack Williams.

glinted most famously in the sunlight as one wore it on the uniform. These badges were manufactured from lead and silver, and when polished to the extreme, would enhance the uniform to a still-further eye-catching level. In some units, this might possibly have been considered "defacement" of these badges, but in the 529th, this level of enhancement was highly encouraged and even rewarded, because it represented a shining image.

And then there were the boots. They received even more special attention. One began this chore ideally with a new pair of "Airborne Jump-boots" – those were the best – and the purchase of anywhere from five to ten regular old tallow candlesticks.

One would then light one of the candles and methodically begin to drip the candlewax onto the toes, heels, and sides of one of the boots. This hot wax would seep into the leather and harden. One would go through this process with a candle or two, then go to a lavatory faucet in one of the bathrooms and run scalding hot water across this boot to remove the wax back down to the leather. Then he'd go back, light a new candlestick, and start the process all over again, dripping more wax.

After going through the first two or

three candles, and then scalding off the excess from the leather surface, most boots would have a good base of wax absorbed into the leather. One next took one last candle and dripped all the wax from it onto this boot, then took it again to the lavatory, except this time, one only allowed the scalding water to slightly melt the wax on the surface of the leather until it was smooth and even, but not completely removed from the boot.

*That was the price one paid for having boots which could be shined each time – with minimal effort thereafter – to a brilliant finish.*

One then would start on the opposite boot in order to allow the first boot to dry and the wax to harden. This entire process would take a day or more. The more candles dripped upon the boots, the more valuable were those boots – and good "candle-waxed boots" were highly prized among Deuce-Niners in the 1970s. (I can't speak for 1960s or later-year Deuce-Niners.)

When completely dry, the waxed toes and heels could then be polished to an incomparable brilliant finish that no drill sergeant could exceed. The image of these boots (and the process was repeated with the black dress shoes worn with the dress-blue uniforms) were the calling card of all Deuce-Niners. The more impressive the boots, the more impressive the trooper.

If someone had a pair of "three-candle boots," that meant that three candles had been melted into each boot, and they were acceptable for use. If someone had a pair of "five-candle" or "eight-candle" boots, however, those were really exceptional, and they'd last not only through that Deuce-Niner's entire tour, but also through the tour of some lucky new owner after that to whom the boots would be passed down.

The only problem with these eye-catching boots was that, in the first few weeks of their use, the experience was roughly equivalent to walking around with blocks of wood tied to one's feet. After being worn for a week or two, however, the boots would begin to "break" naturally at the bend of the toes, and could then be re-polished and shined and worn almost like regular boots – almost...

The good thing about candle-waxed boots was the fact that they could be quickly shined to a brilliant finish each evening for the upcoming new day, but they always retained a certain amount of stiffness which made them moderately uncomfortable to wear. That was the price one paid for having boots which could be shined each time – with minimal effort thereafter – to a brilliant finish.

Some Deuce-Niners went so far as to have "taps" installed on the heels and toes of their boots to reduce wear upon the boot soles and heels. I never wasted the time with those because they were just downright dangerous on those already slippery historic cobblestoned streets found all over Patton and Campbell Barracks and Heidelberg in general.

Another price that one paid for candle-waxed boots was the constantly clogged drains in the washrooms. The wax melted off the boots by the scalding water would obviously drip down into the drains and then harden in the pea-traps of each sink, eventually causing the sink to become unusable. Every few months, after all the lavatories in the washroom had become completely clogged due to candlewax, a plumber had to be summoned to clear the drains. I don't even want to think about what existed farther down in the larger drains in the walls and in the sewers after decades of wax build-up.

To further highlight the appearance of boots and uniform trousers, many Deuce-Niners used what was known as "cans" within the trouser legs to emphasize a perfectly round appearance of "blousing" of the pants cuffs around the top of the boots. These cans came in many different forms and could be made of hard-plastic or even of actual tin cans. These items were also often "inherited" by new troops in the 529th from departing troops.

The administration within the 529th offered "incentives" for one to have a really sharp uniform. Every morning at 5:00 am, the 529th MPs were required to stand for inspection at "Guard Mount" prior to leaving the billets for duty at 6:00 am. That duty usually included 6 to 10 gate-guards (depending upon how many gates were going to be open) each day at Campbell Barracks, the 2 to 4 security personnel at the Command Building, the two guards at the USAREUR Airfield, the 2 to 4 guards at the CINC's quarters in the mountains above Heidelberg, and the 2 gate-guards at Patton Barracks, plus one provisional MP.

Either the duty-officer or the duty-NCOIC (non-commissioned officer-in-charge) closely inspected the uniforms of each MP at Guard Mount to determine which one had the sharpest ("strackest") uniform each morning. The person who was ultimately selected as

"the strackest" was given the day off and the provisional MP would take his place.

In my early days at the 529th, I was only occasionally granted a day-off as a result of my uniform at Guard Mount. Try as I might, I inevitably lost out to one of the "upper-classmen." After winning, they'd inevitably walk away with that little "knowing" smile. As the months passed, however, I learned the tricks of the trade and began winning my share of days off too.

By the time I had been in the Deuce-Nine for six or seven months, I "inherited" a pair of "three-candle" boots from a departing trooper named John Richardson from New Jersey. I eventually could quickly shine those boots to a sparkling finish, and they helped me immensely at Guard-Mount.

The tools of the trade detailed above have been the calling cards of all the troops of the 529th over the years. They were an integral part of what made this MP unit special. In 1974, this excellence was universally recognized when the Deuce-Nine was named as the top military police company in the Army worldwide, an honor in the record books which will stand for many years to come.

On the pages which follow, a sample of the almost endless letters of commendation and recognition presented to the men (and women) of the 529th are displayed in order to provide an inkling of the respect and appreciation engendered toward the Deuce-Nine.

The letters displayed herewith were retained by the author for obvious reasons, but also include recognition for numerous other personnel as well. They represent but a tiny example of the overwhelming admiration demonstrated by military personnel and the general public time and again who witnessed the 1970s-era Deuce-Niners in action.

DEPARTMENT OF THE ARMY
529th MILITARY POLICE COMPANY
APO 09102

14 October 1974

SUBJECT: Letter of Commendation

Specialist Four Ralph O. Jackson
529th Military Police Company
APO 09102

1. The Brigadier General Jeremiah P. Holland Award is presented annually to the most outstanding military police unit, company size or smaller. The criteria utilized for initial nomination and final selection is clearly defined in AR 672-11. Competition for this award is world-wide and highly competitive.

2. On 10 September 1974 this command was officially notified by Headquarters Department of The Army that it was selected as the 1974 recipient of this highly coveted award.

3. During the cited period 1 July 1973 through 30 June 1974, your entire performance of duty, attention to detail and "can do attitude", together with many others assigned to this command, had a significant impact on this unit receiving this award. Your overall contribution to this command has been noted and is sincerely appreciated. You are commended for a job "well done".

4. Take pride in your accomplishments and continue to in all your future endeavors.

5. A copy of this correspondence will be placed in you personnel file.

JAMES W. CASE
Captain, MPC
Commanding

**Heidelberg MP company judged Army's finest**

By JOHN DAVIES

HEIDELBERG — It was one parade the 529th MP Co, USAREUR's honor guard, could get it all together for because it was the company's day to be on the receiving end of recognition and honor.

The Heidelberg-based MPs were formally recognized as the most outstanding MP unit in the Army when Gen. Michael S. Davison, USAREUR and Seventh Army commander-in-chief, presented them with the Army's highest achievement for military police units — the Brig. Gen. Jeremiah P. Holland Award.

Davison presented the award to Capt. James W. Case, 529th commander.

Holland served as USAREUR provost marshal from 1953-1955. He retired in 1957 and subsequently donated the award to be presented each year to that MP unit, company size or smaller, that is determined by the Department of the Army to be the best the Army has to offer.

(22 Jan 74)  2nd Ind
SUBJECT:  Letter of Commendation

Commander, 529th MP Company, APO  09102

TO:  SP4 Ralph O. Jackson, 529th MP Company, APO  09102

1.  You are commended for your exemplary performance of duty while participating in the dedication of the Keyes Building.  You were selected for this dedication because of your constant outstanding performance of duty.

2.  Thank you once again for a job well done and for bringing accolades to this command.

3.  A copy of this correspondence will be placed in your official personnel file.

JAMES W. CASE
Captain, MPC
Commanding

AEUTCO (22 Jan 74) 1st Ind
SUBJECT: Letter of Commendation

Headquarters, USAREUR and Seventh Army Special Troops, APO 09102
29 January 1974

TO: Commander, 529th Military Police Company, APO 09102

1.  I would like to personally add my commendation as well as my
appreciation for the fine performance of Specialists Hansen, Jackson,
and Watson for their participation in the dedication of the Headquarters
Building in honor of General Keyes.

2.  The most outstanding attributes, in addition to those mentioned in
Colonel Adams' letter, were their displayed sensitivity and empathy.
These last two qualities were noted by both General Davison and Mrs.
Desobray.

3.  Please convey to them my personal thanks for a job well done.


                              JOHN J. CASSIDY
                              Colonel, Infantry
                              Commanding

**DEPARTMENT OF THE ARMY**
HEADQUARTERS, UNITED STATES ARMY, EUROPE and SEVENTH ARMY
OFFICE OF THE SECRETARY OF THE GENERAL STAFF
APO 09403

AEAGS

22 January 1974

SUBJECT: Letter of Commendation

TO: Commander
Headquarters USAREUR and Seventh Army Special Troops
APO 09102

1. I would like to commend the personnel of Special Troops who participated in the 17 January ceremony officially renaming the Command Building the Keyes Building in honor of Lieutenant General Keyes.

2. Specialists Donald M. Hansen,                  Ralph O. Jackson, III,
        and Mark D. Watson,                  who participated in
the ceremony, were designated to assist in the unveiling of both the bronze plaque and the oil painting of General Keyes. Their performance in handling their individual responsibilities at a very crucial point in the ceremony in the presence of the large number of distinguished guests was outstanding in every respect.

3. I noted with satisfaction the high standards of appearance of Specialists Hansen, Jackson and Watson. Their uniforms were neat, clean and they presented the proper military appearance. They are to be commended.

4. I desire that Specialists Hansen, Jackson and Watson be appraised of this correspondence as soon as possible.

FLOYD C. ADAMS, JR.
Colonel, GS
Secretary of the General Staff

AEUTA (22 Nov 74) 1st Ind
SUBJECT: Letter of Commendation

Commander, Headquarters, USAREUR and Seventh Army Special Troops   APO 09102
9 Dec 74

THRU:   Commander, 529th Military Police Company, USAREUR and Seventh Army
        Special Troops   APO 09102

TO:     Specialist Four Ralph O. Jackson, 529th Military Police Company,
        USAREUR and Seventh Army Special Troops   APO 09102

1.  It is a pleasure for me to forward the commendatory remarks of
Colonel Floyd C. Adams, Jr.

2.  Your outstanding performance of duty brings much credit upon you,
your unit and the United States Army.  You are commended for a job
well done.

                                        JOHN J. CASSIDY
                                        Colonel, Infantry
                                        Commanding

**DEPARTMENT OF THE ARMY**
HEADQUARTERS, UNITED STATES ARMY, EUROPE and SEVENTH ARMY
OFFICE OF THE SECRETARY OF THE GENERAL STAFF
APO 09403

AEAGS

22 November 1974

SUBJECT: Letter of Commendation

THRU:     Commander
          Headquarters, US Army, Europe
            and Seventh Army Special Troops
          APO  09102

TO:       Specialist Four Ralph O. Jackson

          529th Military Police Company
          APO  09102

1.  The purpose of this letter is to commend you for your performance of duty for the period during which you were assigned to Headquarters, United States Army, Europe.

2.  Your performance while working in the Keyes Building as a member of the Security Guard Force was exemplary.  I am deeply appreciative of your professional dedication to duty and spirit of cooperation demonstrated during the daily accomplishment of your mission.  Your quiet enthusiasm and attention to detail contributed significantly toward providing reliable security to the building and personnel of the Command Group, Headquarters, US Army, Europe.

3.  I wish you continued success in your future endeavors. A copy of this correspondence will be placed in your official Army records.

                              FLOYD C. ADAMS, JR.
                              Colonel, GS
                              Secretary of the General Staff

Amazing "Esprit de Corps"

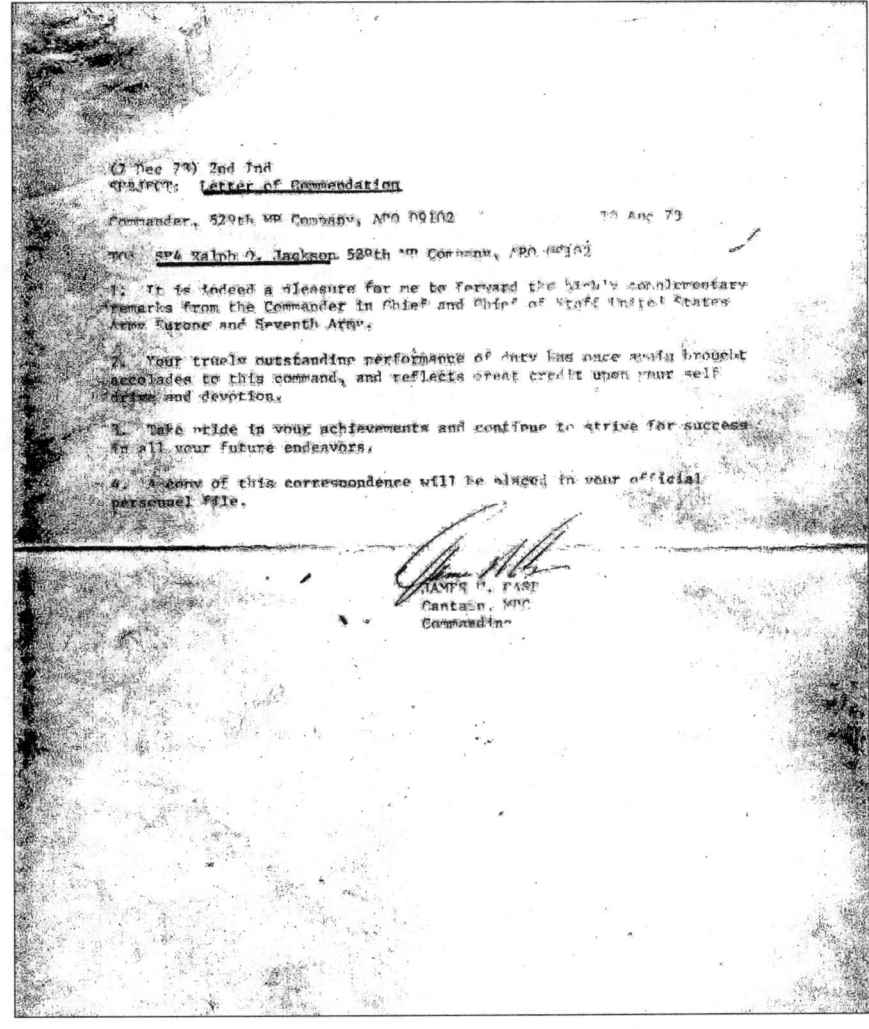

(7 Dec 79) 2nd Ind
SUBJECT: Letter of Commendation

Commander, 529th MP Company, APO 09102                    30 Aug 79

TO: SP4 Ralph O. Jackson 529th MP Company, APO 09102

1. It is indeed a pleasure for me to forward the high's complimentary remarks from the Commander in Chief and Chief of Staff United States Army Europe and Seventh Army.

2. Your truely outstanding performance of duty has once again brought accolades to this command, and reflects great credit upon your self drive and devotion.

3. Take pride in your achievements and continue to strive for success in all your future endeavors.

4. A copy of this correspondence will be placed in your official personnel file.

                              JAMES C. FAST
                              Captain, MPC
                              Commanding

35

AEUTSO (27 Nov 73) 1st Ind
SUBJECT: Letter of Commendation

HQ, USAREUR & Seventh Army Special Troops, APO 09102
7 Dec 73

TO: Commander, 529th MP Co, APO 09102

1. It is a pleasure for me to forward the laudatory remarks of Major General William R. Kraft, Jr.

2. The outstanding performance of the USAREUR Color Guard during the Project Partnership Ceremony in Neu Ulm has contributed tremendously towards strengthening and maintaining our relations with the host nation. Please pass on to each individual in the Color Guard my thanks and appreciation for the outstanding professionalism displayed.

Donald Wierzema
Jack Williams
Kyle Harris
Randall Roberts
R.O. Jackson

for JOHN J. CASSIDY
Colonel, Infantry
Commanding

**DEPARTMENT OF THE ARMY**
HEADQUARTERS, UNITED STATES ARMY, EUROPE and SEVENTH ARMY
APO 09403

AEAGS                                             27 November 1973

SUBJECT: Letter of Commendation

THRU:   Commander
        Headquarters, United States Army,
          Europe and Seventh Army Special Troops
        APO 09403

TO:     Commander
        529th Military Police Company
        APO 09102

1. The Commander in Chief has noted with pleasure the outstanding performance of the USAREUR Color Guard during the Project Partnership Ceremony at Neu Ulm on 15 November 1973, and has asked me to express his commendation for this exceptional display of professionalism.

2. The importance of professionalism and performance at an event such as this cannot be overstated, for it not only strengthens the USAREUR image before numerous citizens of our host nation, but also reinforces the credibility of our dedication and resolve. Further, and perhaps just as importantly, it strengthens the bonds of friendship which have characterized our relations with the German people from the very beginning of the alliance.

3. I add my commendation to that of General Davison and ask that you express his appreciation to the members of the Color Guard for their impressive performance. The conscientious manner in which they performed their duties reflects most favorably upon the United States Army and this command.

Spec-4 Donald Wierzema
Spec-4 Jack Williams
Spec-4 Kyle Harris                          WILLIAM R. KRAFT, JR.
Sgt. Randall Roberts                        Major-General, GS
Spec-4 R.O. Jackson                         Chief of Staff

(26 October 1973) 1st Ind
SUBJECT: Letter of Appreciation

Commander, 529th MP Company, APO 09102

TO: SP4 Ralph D. Jackson, 529th MP Company, APO 09102

1. It is indeed a pleasure to forward the laudatory comments of the Special Troops Command Sergeant Major.

2. Take pride in your accomplishments and continue to strive for success in your future endeavors.

3. A copy of this correspondence will be placed in your official personnel file.

JAMES W. CASE
Captain, MPC
Commanding

**DEPARTMENT OF THE ARMY**
HEADQUARTERS, USAREUR AND SEVENTH ARMY SPECIAL TROOPS
APO 09102

AEUTCSM                                    26 October 1973

SUBJECT: Letter of Appreciation

Specialist Fourth Class Ralph O. Jackson

529th Military Police Company
APO 09102

1. I wish to express my sincere appreciation for the time and effort which you contributed towards making the 1973 Formal Noncommissioned Officers' Ball on 19 October 1973 an outstanding success.

2. The performance of the members of the Honor Guard was truly outstanding. The military precision exhibited by you reflected the many hours of rehearsal and hard work necessary for a high level of performance and was greatly enjoyed by all the guests.

3. I commend you for a job well done.

SAMUEL E. ADAMS
CSM, USA
USAREUR/7A Special Troops

(3 Oct 73) 2nd Ind
SUBJECT: Letter of Appreciation

Commander, 529th MP Company, APO 09102          10 October 1973

TO:  SP4 Ralph O. Jackson, 529th MP Company, APO 09102

1. It gives me great pleasure to forward laudatory comments from
the USAREUR Provost Marshal and from the Special Troops Commander
regarding your performance of duty at the 32nd Military Police Anniversary
Ball. I too was present and witnessed the highly professional, precision
movements of the USAREUR Color Guard, of which you are apart.

2. Additionally, once again on 27 September 1973 you posted the colors
at "our" unit party. All of "us" in the 529th were proud of you.

3. Take pride in your accomplishments and continue to strive for success
in all your future endeavors.

4. A copy of this correspondence will be placed in your official
personnel records.

JAMES W. CASE
Captain, MPC
Commanding

AEUTA (27 Sept 73) 1st Ind
SUBJECT: Letter of Appreciation

DA, Headquarters USAREUR & Seventh Army Special Troops, APO 09102    3 October

TO:  Color Guard, 529th Military Police Company, APO 09102

1.  I am pleased to forward the appreciative remarks of Brigadier General
Paul M. Timmerberg concerning your outstanding performance at the Military
Police Anniversary Ball on 21 September 1973.

2.  Please convey my thanks to SSG Patrick B. Mackay, SP4 Kyle W. Harris, SP4
Ralph O. Jackson, SP4 Danny R. Norman, and SP4 Jack R. Williams for their
demonstrated professionalism.

JOHN J. CASSIDY
Colonel, Infantry
Commanding

**DEPARTMENT OF THE ARMY**

HEADQUARTERS, UNITED STATES ARMY, EUROPE and SEVENTH ARMY
OFFICE OF THE PROVOST MARSHAL
APO 09403

AEAPM

27 September 1973

SUBJECT: Letter of Appreciation

THRU: Commander
USAREUR and Seventh Army Special Troops
APO 09102

Commander
529th MP Company
APO 09102

TO: Color Guard
529th MP Company
APO 09102

1. On behalf of all in attendance, appreciation is expressed for your outstanding performance while posting and retiring the colors in the MP Anniversary Ball on 21 September 1973. The professionalism you displayed set the tone for a most enjoyable Anniversary Celebration.

2. To each, SSG Patrick B. Mackay, SP4 Kyle W. Harris, SP4 Ralph O. Jackson SP4 Danny R. Norman, and SP4 Jack R. Williams, a special thank you. Your performance reflected credit upon yourselves, your unit and the Military Police Corps.

PAUL M. TIMMERBERG
Brigadier General, USA
Provost Marshal

(9 Jul 73) 2nd Ind
SUBJECT: Letter of Appreciation

529th Military Police Company, APO 09102, 19 July 1973

TO: SP4 Ralph O. Jackson, 529th Military Police Company, APO 09102

1. It is with great pleasure that I forward the laudatory remarks from the Commander, 42nd Customs Group regarding your performance at the change of command ceremony.

2. Once again your professionalism and attention to detail has been noted. You are indeed a valuable asset to this command.

3. A copy of this correspondence will be placed in your official file.

JAMES W. CASE
Captain, MPC
Commanding

**DEPARTMENT OF THE ARMY**
HEADQUARTERS, 42D MILITARY POLICE GROUP (CUSTOMS)
APO 09403

AEUMP-CO                                                        9 July 1973

SUBJECT: Letter of Appreciation          Donald Wierzema
                                          Jack Williams
                                          Kyle Harris
                                          Randall Roberts
THRU: Commander                           R.O. Jackson
      USAREUR & 7A Special Troops
      APO 09102

TO:   Commander
      529th MP Company
      APO 09102

1.  It is with a great deal of pleasure that I take this opportunity
to personally thank you for your support by permitting the color
guard personnel to perform during my recent change of command ceremony
here at the 42d MP Group (Customs).

2.  Your personnel assisted in making this ceremony more meaningful
to me by their outstanding performance. Without exception, all personnel exhibited traits of professionalism and Esprit de Corps which
certainly reflects on your unit.

3.  Thank you again for your assistance and please make my feelings
known to these fine men.

                              ROBERT W. HOOKER
                              COL, MPC
                              Commanding

AEUTCO (15 Jun 73) 1st Ind
SUBJECT: Letter of Appreciation

DA, HQ USAREUR and Seventh Army Special Troops, APO 09102
25 June 1973

TO: Commander, 529th Military Police Company, APO 09102

Please express my appreciation to each of your men who participated
in this event and made it a success. You can be proud of each one of
them. Thank you for a job well done.

RICHARD E. HOERNING
Lieutenant Colonel, FA
Acting Commander

AEUTDCO (11 Jun 73) 1st Ind
SUBJECT: Letter of Appreciation

DA, HQ USAREUR and Seventh Army Special Troops, APO 09102
13 June 1973

TO: Commander, 529th Military Police Company, APO 09102

Please relay these congratulatory remarks to those personnel who participated in this event. Their performance is in keeping with the high standards of your unit and the U. S. Army. Thank you for a job well done.

FOR THE COMMANDER:

RICHARD E. HOERNING
Lieutenant Colonel, FA
Deputy Commander

DEPARTMENT OF THE ARMY
Heidelberg Military Police Station
APO 09102

AEZMP-KA-H                                                    26 July 72

SUBJECT:  Letter of Appreciation


THRU:  Commanding Officer
       529th Military Police Company
       APO 09102

TO  :  PFC JACKSON, Ralph O.

       529th MP Co
       APO 09102


I would like to take this opportunity to express my appreciation to you
for the excellent support rendered to this station during the 1972
American Volksfest.

The professional manner in which you accomplished your duties was commend-
able.  Continued performance of this type can only serve to mark you as an
outstanding Military Policeman.  I sincerely appreciate your outstanding
attitude and your conscientiousness.

                                   JAMES F. WESTERBERG
                                   CPT, MPC
                                   Station Commander

47

## Chapter 6

# The Terrorist Attack of 1972

The year 1972 in Heidelberg, West Germany, would usher in one of the most momentous events of the past quarter-century, setting the stage for exceptionally unusual and emergency circumstances within the 529th Military Police Company for years into the future.

On May 24th, 1972, two female German nationals drove two vehicles with stolen United States Army – Europe (USAREUR) license plates through the front gate of the USAREUR complex at Campbell Barracks in Heidelberg. At that time, the fact that the vehicles had USAREUR license plates provided them with an automatic "entre'" into the otherwise secure facility. That was the security policy at that time. It was a flaw in the system, but as far as the official military security staff at Heidelberg were concerned, there simply was no need for excessively-strict security measures – at least so they thought. They were about to be rudely awakened to the deadly reality of a growing phenomenon.

The decade of the 1970s in Germany would become one of the most dangerous periods for the U.S. Army since World War II. In the four years from 1970 to 1974 alone, 129 deadly acts of terrorism against the United States Army occurred in Germany. From 1970 to 1980, there were 312 acts of terrorism committed against the Army. Though little-known at the time and little-realized by most Americans today, a native

element in Germany – much composed of the children and grandchildren of former NAZI Germany officials – had made it their goal in life to uproot the American military in their country.

It would later be learned that both of the falsely-authorized vehicles allowed into Campbell Barracks in Heidelberg on May 24, 1972, contained immense improvised explosive devices (IEDs). One of the vehicles was driven back to the vicinity of the ivy-covered Officers' Club in the rear of Campbell and parked next to a yellow Ford Capri in the large parking area. The other vehicle was parked a short distance away beside the USAREUR response and command center known in Army parlance as "the war room."

The Campbell Barracks Officers' Club at that time was a very popular area in which officers and their families often converged in the evenings and on weekends for meals and light-hearted family gatherings. A movie theater next door provided further incentive to visit this area. I often visited this area myself, particularly to enjoy the latest first-run movies.

Later investigations by the U.S. Army Criminal Investigation Division (CID) would reveal that at about 6:00 pm, Capt. Clyde Bonner, a twenty-nine years old officer in the Army who was married with two children, invited his friend – Ronald Woodward who was also married with three children – to

Campbell Barracks on Romerstrasse in the center of this photo is easily identifiable by the large parade field and center flagpole. The explosives from the 1972 terrorist attack were detonated in the parking lot to the rear of the building just beyond the parade field. Constructed in 1937 in what then was Nazi Germany, this facility (later known as "Campbell Barracks") was originally named "Grenadier Kaserne" (just as were the structures built in what later became known as "Patton Barracks" on nearby Kircheimer Weg), and was designed to house contingents of the Wehrmacht's 110th Infantry Regiment. When completed, both facilities were known collectively as "Grenadier Kaserne." The Romerstrasse facility became the home of the 110th Infantry Regiment's headquarters, its 1st Battalion, and its two regimental support companies. The Kircheimer Weg facility (later Patton) housed the regiment's 3rd Battalion.

come see his brand-new yellow Ford Capri out in the parking lot. Bonner's pride in the vehicle was obvious that day, but the decision of the two men to go examine it was a fateful one.

At two minutes past 6:00 pm, as the two men were admiring the bright yellow sports car, the IED hidden in the vehicle parked immediately beside Bonner's Capri detonated. The resulting explosion was absolutely devastating and horrifying. It tossed vehicles and

their contents like matchsticks around the parking lot and turned an otherwise organized parking system into a large expanse of absolute chaos.

According to the official Army Criminal Investigation Division (CID) report, the detonation instantly ripped all the clothing – including boots – from Bonner's body, and dismembered it into numerous portions which were strewn throughout the parking lot. Boots, clothing, and various and sundry other

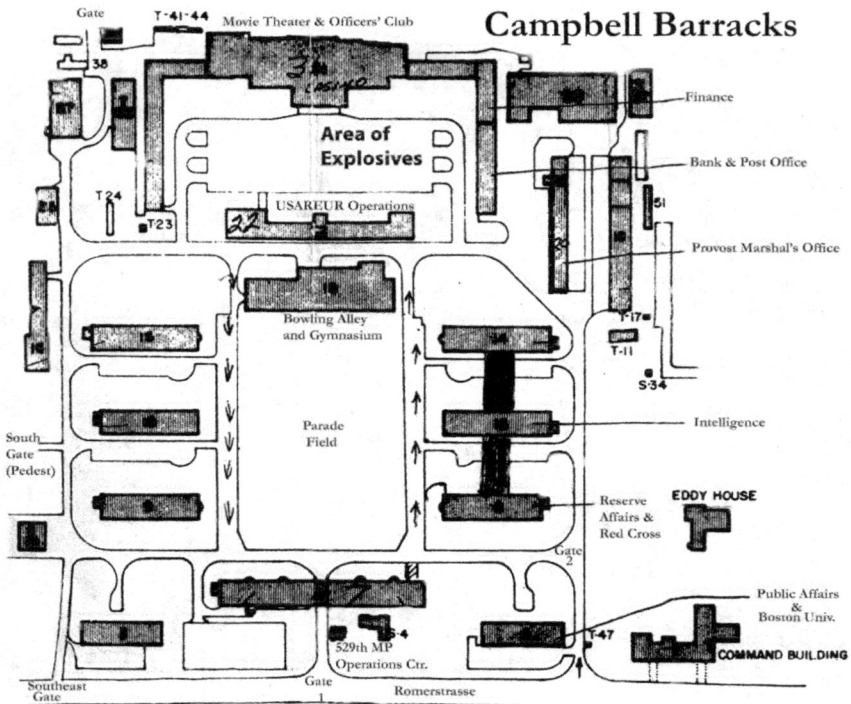

This schematic indicates most of the USAREUR offices and other incidentals once located at Campbell Barracks when it was the site of USAREUR headquarters in Europe. It also indicates the general area in which the explosives from the 1972 terrorist attack at Campbell Barracks were detonated. (Schematic courtesy of Bob Walls.)

small items from the blast victims were discovered hanging from nearby trees for weeks thereafter. Woodward was killed just as instantly, and though the blast tore off and scattered his clothing as well, his body was somehow shielded to some degree so that, according to the report, the blast did not destroy his corpse.

Approximately 15 seconds later, a second detonation – equally horrendous – occurred in the other vehicle nearby, doubling the chaos now filling the parking lot and Officers' Club. The War Room was an ultra-high security complex, the existence of which was not supposed to have been common knowledge. Interior security for these offices was

provided by contingents of the 529th MP Company who had no less than a "Secret Intelligence" clearance – the highest security clearance available at that time.

As a result, it is still debated today how the terrorists were able to gain knowledge of the existence of the War Room complex. Perhaps they did not even know of it at all and the placement of the IED in that vicinity was happenstance. The answer to that – as well as many other questions concerning this event – will probably never be known.

Inside the Command and Control facility, further CID investigative reports indicated Charles Peck died when a soft-drink dispenser – driven by the

A military policeman from the 529th MP Company walks past damaged cars at the United States Army Europe (USAREUR) headquarters command in Heidelberg, West Germany on May 24, 1972. Two improvised explosive devices were detonated in a parking area inside USAREUR's Campbell Barracks shortly after 6:00 p.m. Three individuals were killed and numerous others were injured in the blast. According to one investigator, had the devices been detonated an hour or more earlier, there would have been untold numbers of additional casualties.

force of the blast from the terrorists' car parked outside – slammed the dispenser into him, crushing him against an adjacent wall. I will never forget the bloody handprints Peck left upon that wall where he apparently had attempted either to rise following the blast or, perhaps simply to catch himself after being flung against the wall and crushed by the soft-drink container. Whatever the circumstances, Peck was simply too badly injured, and the two bloody smears from his hands sliding down the wall to the floor where he had collapsed and died clearly indicated the story of his demise.

The bomb blasts – despite the fact that they occurred from vehicles parked in the outside parking lot – were unbelievably devastating. Vehicles in the vicinity of the two IED-laden vehicles were tossed and crushed like soda cans. A portion of the parking lot was a virtual jungle of twisted and destroyed vehicles – some lying atop others – whose contents had been obliterated and strewn as well across the cobble-stoned expanse of the parking lot.

The explosives were later determined to have been in the 50 to 60-pound bomb range. They had been planted where they of course would render maximum damage, killing not only United States military personnel, but the wives and children of these personnel, the German workers inside the compound, and anyone else unfortunate enough to be within range of the explosives. One can only consider it an act of God that no more than three individuals died from their injuries on this terrible evening. Numerous other persons were injured by flying glass and debris.

Had the second detonation been timed to explode 15 or 20 minutes (instead of only 3 or 4 minutes) after the first explosion when crowds of the survivors had begun emerging from the Officers' Club and theater and running and staggering across the parking lot, there undoubtedly would have been far more deaths. Again, there but for the grace of God were many further casualties avoided.

When the detonations occurred, the front gate-guard at Campbell was shocked beyond description at the horrendous blasts. When the initial explosion was triggered, the guard leapt into the air and almost fell, such was his shock. As he walked slowly in disbelief toward the opening beneath the large building at the front gate, peering into the distance, the second explosion occurred, shocking him even further as debris began raining down upon the parade field.

The guard subsequently ran into the 529th Operations Center 45 to 50 feet away and began yelling at the 529th desk sergeant that Campbell was being bombed. As both men ran back out into the street to look back across the Campbell Parade Field toward the source of the blasts, a large cloud of debris began gathering over the parade field. Though the horrendous concussive effect of the blasts was more than enough evidence of an emergency situation, when they saw the smoke, dust and debris filling the air above and raining down upon the compound, they knew the circumstances were indeed dire.

The desk sergeant then ran back inside the Operations Center and picked up the Emergency Line to the duty officer back at Patton Barracks and hurriedly filled him in on the details. This duty officer in turn notified the duty officer at the Command (Keyes) Building down the street in order to activate an even larger alert and alarm.

Emergency medical technicians, personnel from the Army CID, 529th and 536th Military Police companies, as well as elements of the German civilian police began arriving quite quickly at the scene of what most everyone now was certain was an intentional act of terrorism. Some shocked and injured civilians and U.S. Army personnel also began streaming out of the gate toward the 529th Operations Center, many of them in shock and explaining that huge explosions had occurred.

Meanwhile, back at Patton Barracks approximately one mile away (as the crow flies across country), the men of the 529th were well aware that an emergency situation existed. The shock-wave of the blasts had rattled the buildings and sent some of the older veterans at Patton immediately to the Orderly Room for further instruction.

Patrol units from the 529th were quickly dispatched to Campbell. All existing NCOs and officers living off-post were immediately summoned, and additional emergency personnel were organized.

Since there were many personnel injured, confused, and now stranded without vehicles at the Officers' Club and movie theater – though the situation warranted an initial examination by explosives experts – emergency personnel nevertheless advanced immediately into the area of the blasts. The heinous and evil nature of the attack would have been compounded had there been any further explosives set to detonate during this time of rescue, but luckily such was not the case.

A slew of ruined vehicles litter the parking lot adjacent to the Officers' Club at Campbell Barracks in Heidelberg following the May 24, 1972 terrorist attack. A group known as the Red Brigades took credit for the incident which killed three American servicemen and seriously injured five other individuals. (AP Photo)

Once it was determined that it was safe to examine the scene, a massive investigation was organized. The area was roped and sealed off by CID and MPs from the 529th and 536th MP companies, and the task of an extensive forensics investigation and the identification and removal of the bodies, began in earnest. Injured personnel were removed to the Army's 130th Station Hospital just up Romerstrasse.

The Heidelberg terrorist attack was only one of numerous similar bombings in the early 1970s which targeted U.S. military installations. Other attack sites included Augsburg, Munich, Karlsruhe, Hamburg, Berlin, and Frankfurt just to name a few. It had suddenly become exceedingly dangerous to be located on a U.S. Army base in Germany. Some of the major incidents during this time included:

**Attack on the Munich Airport, February 10, 1970**: Three terrorists attacked El Al passengers in a bus at the Munich Airport with guns and grenades. One passenger was killed and 11 were injured. All three terrorists were captured by airport police. The Action Organization for the Liberation of Palestine and the Popular Democratic Front for the Liberation of Palestine claimed responsibility for this attack.

**Attack on a Frankfurt U.S. Army Officers Club, May 11, 1972**: An Army lieutenant colonel was killed and 13 persons injured when three bombs shattered a Fifth Corps headquarters officers' club in Frankfurt, Germany.

**Massacre at the Munich Olympic Village, September 5, 1972**: Eight Palestinian "Black September" terrorists seized eleven Israeli athletes in the Olympic Village in Munich, West Germany. In a bungled rescue attempt by West German authorities, nine of the hostages and five terrorists were subsequently murdered.

In the months over the next two years, it was discovered from investigations that a majority of the attacks inside Germany were being committed by a group of extreme radical socialist leftists known as the "Red Army Faction," or "Baader-Meinhof Terrorists." As it turned out, most of the individuals involved in these acts of terrorism, interestingly, were, as explained above, the children or grandchildren of former Nazi officials who had made it their mission in life to oust the American military from Germany by force, using fear as a motivational factor.

The Baader-Meinhof terrorist group included many different individuals, but the primary leaders were Gudrun Ensslin, Andreas Baader, Ulrike Meinhoff, Irene Goergens, Ingrid Schubert, Angela Luther, Irmgard Moeller and Holger Meins among others.

Moeller and Luther were ultimately determined to have been the individuals heartless enough to plant the explosives inside Campbell Barracks. They were not captured that day, remaining at large for a number of weeks. They, however, had been described to Army CID officials by several individuals who had witnessed their suspicious behavior following the parking of their bomb-laden vehicles inside Campbell.

Both Moeller and Luther were ultimately captured by German law enforcement personnel and paid for their crimes. That, however, did nothing for the loved ones of their victims – Bonner, Woodward, and Peck.

Following the May 24, 1972 incident, the men of the 529th took pride in the fact that Gen. Michael S. Davison, the CINC at that time and his staff had not been endangered on that day, nor was he ever endangered prior to his retirement from the Army in 1975. His successor, however, was not so fortunate.

After being placed on "alert status," the 529th Military Police Company was fully mobilized. No one was granted leave of any type, nor any type of interruptive behavior whatsoever.

In the hours, days and weeks thereafter, there would be no such thing as a vehicle passing into Patton or Campbell Barracks without an intense examination not only of the identity of the individual(s) in the vehicle, but also of the vehicle itself for explosives. Anyone not in possession of the proper identity credentials were barred from the compounds.

As a result, thereafter, on the weekday mornings, a line of daily commuters snaked for a mile or more down Romerstrasse (an ancient Roman road through Heidelberg) outside Campbell Barracks. The traffic into Patton Barracks was equally delayed and frustrated while the 529th cautiously and tediously checked each vehicle and its occupants.

During this time, the patience of those in need of access to these two facilities ran thin and tempers often flared, but the intensive searches continued unabated. U.S. military personnel in uniform with proper U.S. military identification credentials and USAREUR license plates on their vehicles, however, were generally admitted without much delay.

The U.S. military, in conjunction with the German law enforcement community, eventually ferreted out numerous members of the Red Army Faction in Europe, decimating their membership. Following their imprisonment, some of these individuals committed suicide rather than spend the remainder of their days in prison.

It took several weeks for the investigation of the blast sites at Campbell to be fully completed. During that time and for several weeks thereafter, the 529th was responsible for securing the site, and setting up a perimeter patrol on a 24-hour basis. I'll never forget the smell of death which lingered in the vicinity of this site for weeks thereafter.

## Chapter 7

The Terrorist Attack of 1981

The decade of the 1970s was barely in the record books when, in September of 1981, just a little over nine years after the tragic 1972 Campbell Barracks terrorist incident in Heidelberg, yet another terrorist cell unleashed yet another direct assault upon the 529th. Gen. Davison's successor as the USAREUR CINC in Heidelberg – Gen. Frederick Kroesen, also a four-star – was the victim in this instance, and it was the first such incident in which the CINC was actually personally threatened and injured.

The shady heavily forested stretches with thick undergrowth along the mountain lane from the CINC's mountain residence down to Heidelberg had long been known to be a dangerous stretch of lonely road ideally-suited for possible ambush opportunities for terrorists. During the 1970s, Gen. Davison, surprisingly, eschewed practically any type of protective services for himself on the daily drive on this stretch down the mountain to his offices at the Command Building some six or eight miles away. As it turned out, he was quite fortuitous.

In 1979, after Gen. Kroesen – Davison's successor as CINC – had taken up the mantle of leadership of the United States Army in Europe, he had become more cautious out of necessity. Terrorist attacks had become so insidious by that point that he had deemed it prudent to ride daily with a protective security detail of MPs from the 529th.

On the day of the attack in September of 1981, General Kroesen's limousine had exited the CINC's residence in the early morning as usual, and proceeded with its MP escort down the mountain headed toward the Command Building in Heidelberg. Suddenly, just as had been predicted, the general and his escort found themselves under a heavy assault from both rocket-propelled antitank grenade (RPG) and automatic weapons fire. The attackers were hidden in a camouflaged blind deep in the forest cover alongside the road.

An initial RPG struck the General's vehicle in the rear trunk area with a deafening roar. It destroyed much of the rear of the Mercedes-Benz sedan, right up to the rear seat in which the General and his wife were seated, but the vehicle's chasis remained intact so that the sedan remained drivable. Had the vehicle not been equipped with extra armor plating around the passenger compartment – a precaution which had only recently been taken due to the now frequent terrorist attacks being imposed upon U.S. Army personnel – the resulting damage undoubtedly would have been far greater, and the injuries to those inside the vehicle would have been much more serious – if not fatal.

It is still unknown today why the fuel tank of the vehicle did not ignite. Had this occurred, it almost certainly would also have caused fatalities in this incident, but fortune smiled in that regard as well

The narrow mountain road – with its dark forests and thick undergrowth – leading down from the CINC-USAREUR's residence to his offices at the Command Building in Heidelberg had been identified as a possible area of ambush by terrorists. In 1981, quite near the site pictured here on this route, opportunistic assassins used rocket-propelled grenades (RPGs) and automatic weapons to make an attempt upon the life of Gen. Kroessen who had replaced Gen. Davison as CINC upon his retirement. The beautiful and contrastingly peaceful Neckar River with its scenic river cruises today is visible in the distance below. (Photo by R.O. Jackson)

upon those in Kroesen's sedan. It was reasoned by some that the fuel tank did not ignite due to the fact that the RPG round struck horizontally across the top of the rear trunk area (shearing off the trunk) instead of longitudinally (from rear to front) on the vehicle.

When the RPG struck his vehicle, Gen. Kroesen's driver quickly did everything in his power to move the vehicle out of range of the assault unit. Though they believed they might have escaped with their lives at that point, those in Kroesen's vehicle suddenly realized that not only had yet another RPG been fired at them, but that they were now taking automatic weapons fire from the terrorists which was striking the vehicle as it careened down the mountain road.

Though the automatic weapons fire was finding the mark on the vehicle, the second RPG fortunately went wide,

missing the sedan. The MP escort vehicle which had pulled up protectively to the rear of the General's sedan amazingly was not struck at all by RPG rounds or automatic weapons fire.

Though the MPs of the 529th had drawn their weapons, by the time they might have returned fire upon the attackers, they had already advanced too far down the road and around a curve. They also reasoned, wisely as it turned out, that it would have been foolish to pit two MPs with side-arms against an obviously-determined foe with not only powerfully-destructive RPG assault weapons, but also automatic rifles as well.

When it suddenly became evident that the general had been wounded, the driver proceeded immediately to the 130th Station Hospital in Heidelberg. Gen. Kroesen had been struck from the rear not by RPG round fragments (which almost certainly would have been fatal), but by the shattered glass and small shards of shredded metal from his vehicle's rear window, and was bleeding heavily from his head and neck. His wife, Rowene, had also been injured, but not to the degree of her husband.

*"The glass on the back window shattered, and I was thrown forward from the blast,"* Kroesen later stated. *"It* (the glass) *cut me all over the back of my head. My wife looked over at me, and she thought I was dead, because she thought that the whole back of my head had been blown off."*

Rowene Kroesen had accompanied her husband on this fateful day due, ironically, to a dental appointment. It was a medical necessity which she ultimately rued. She, just as her husband, was cut by the flying glass and shards of metal thrown off by the RPG round and automatic weapons fire, but not nearly as seriously as her husband. No one else was injured.

Later investigations revealed the blind used by the terrorist attackers was located in a thickly-wooded area of the hillside about 200 yards from Kroesen's vehicle. According to the investigators at the scene, the second RPG round which had missed them had cut a foot-deep gash into the pavement approximately two yards beyond them – far too close for comfort.

MPs from the 529th and Army Criminal Investigation Division (CID) officials discovered a tent equipped with a radio transmitter, sleeping bags and food, indicating the terrorists were well-supplied and had spent the night in the area awaiting their quarry. With the discovery of the transmitter, it was speculated that the terrorists had positioned a spotter higher up on the mountain to alert those farther down of Kroesen's imminent approach.

Following the attack, a witness later reported seeing a fleeing individual climbing up a rope onto a cliff and then running away from the scene of the attack. The cell appeared to be well-organized and arms specialists at the scene marveled at the fact that the attackers had been able to successfully strike the swiftly-moving vehicle with one RPG round and narrowly missed it with a second.

I can't help reflecting that nine years earlier in 1972, Gen. Davison had insisted upon jogging unprotected up that same mountain road and being driven daily down it unescorted in a vehicle without any armor plating or MP protection whatsoever. His life could easily have been in jeopardy. *(Readers please see "Protecting the CINC" in this volume.)*

The MPs at the 529th, nevertheless, were very cautious within the parameters of the tools and orders under which they functioned, especially when directly responsible for the CINC's protection at his residence, the Command Building, or anywhere else. When the dangerous terrorist climate – which continued throughout the decade of the 1970s in Germany – became even worse as the decade progressed, the security measures for the CINC were re-doubled and enhanced considerably.

Effective protection and good fortune rode with Gen. Davison in the 1970s in Heidelberg, just as it had in World War II, the Korean War, and Vietnam Conflict. His life seemed blessed.

And in 1981, despite his injuries, Gen. Kroesen – a World War II, Korean and Vietnam wars veteran as well – was equally blessed to have avoided serious injury in Germany. From that point forward, no attacks on the CINC or his personnel have been forth-coming in Germany, though a vigilant watch has been continuously maintained ever since.

## Chapter 8

# Honor Guard Burial Ceremonies for WWII Casualties

A portion of the duty at the 529$^{th}$ involved honor guard details. This meant dressing in our fitted dress blue uniforms and being assigned M-14 ceremonial rifles (sometimes with blank rounds for 21-gun salutes) for official honor guard ceremonies. In these events, the national and U.S. Army flags were paraded, formation marches and passes-in-review to honor a United States or foreign dignitary were conducted, the "Colors" were presented, or special burial ceremonies were provided for fallen soldiers.

On one occasion in 1972, a farmer in Belgium had been clearing a dense forest in order to cultivate additional acreage when he discovered remains from World War II. This was not unusual since fallen soldiers – from both sides – were often discovered, and are still occasionally encountered even today.

In the early 1970s, it had barely been 25 years since the end of that great conflict. The detritus of war often obscured remains ultimately recovered from the debris. More often than not, when this occurred, the skills of the 529$^{th}$ were summoned to provide a respectful, dignified, and impressive burial ceremony for the deceased.

On a foggy, overcast day in 1972, a detail from the 529th Military Police Company Honor Guard provides ceremonial duties at a military burial for a soldier from World War II whose body had been discovered in a dense wooded area in the nearby Ardennes Forest. This burial site is the Ardennes American Cemetery and Memorial twelve miles southwest of Liege, Belgium. The soldier had been one of a number of bodies discovered at a crash site of one of the many gliders used to send troops behind the German lines during the final year of World War II in Europe.

After the authorities were notified of the discovery of the soldiers' remains in the Belgium forest, forensics experts confirmed them to be those of American crewmen from one of the many glider planes flown into Germany sometime in

With his duty completed, the last remains of the departed are provided a 21-gun salute by the 529th Honor Guard, after which the always poignant "Taps" was sounded by the bugler in the distance.

1944, when U.S. troops used these craft to silently slip behind enemy lines unnoticed.

This particular crew had either been spotted by enemy aircraft and shot down, or else had simply all died from injuries after their wooden glider had crashed into the dense forest. Whatever the circumstances, it is believed that all the men in this craft perished during the chaos of 1944, and their remains had lain undiscovered until 1972.

The crewmen were identified by their dog-tags. Their next-of-kin were subsequently notified of their discovery so that they might have closure with the deceased and attend the burial ceremony if they so chose.

A detail from the 529th was selected to travel to the Ardennes American Cemetery and Memorial twelve miles southwest of Liege, Belgium, where the remains were officially buried in marked graves. A 21-gun salute was provided for the fallen soldiers and "Taps" was played before the remains were laid to rest.

The performance of official ceremonial 21-gun salutes and honor guard ceremonies at the burials of veterans was just one of the many and varied responsibilities of the 529th. Though our primary mission was the security and protection of the commander-in-chief of the U.S. Army in Europe, his offices and staff, a secondary role – which was almost as important – involved the official honor guard ceremonies for the Army.

*A 21-gun salute was provided for the fallen soldiers and "Taps" was played before the remains were laid to rest.*

# Chapter 9

# Colorful "Personalities"

The late Jerry Clower, a hilarious stand-up comic from the 1980s-1990s, was immensely popular on the comedy-club circuit back in the day, and reminded me somewhat of the twisted humor which often prevailed within the ranks of the 529th at Patton Barracks in Heidelberg.

One of Clower's skits involved two hunters, one of whom had wounded a large bobcat which had escaped into the brushy confines of a tall pine tree late one night. According to Clower's skit, the hunter ascended the tree to run the wounded animal back to ground, but ran into a bit more than he could handle.

Long story short, after the tree's branches had shaken violently for several minutes and howls of pain had erupted on and off from the shadowy confines of the treetop, and after the hunting partner still on the ground had been unable to see the bobcat to shoot it, the climbing hunter up in the heights of the tree eventually yelled quite desperately down to his partner on the ground with the urgent plea to *"Just shoot up here amongst us and give one of us some relief!"*

It was dark humor such as this which often-times prevailed at the 529th. Despite the intense nature of the security mission of the 529th Military Police Company – particularly in the months following the May 24, 1972 terrorist incident at Campbell Barracks – things began returning to a semblance of normality in six or eight months.

In an environment such as this, young men – even military policemen charged with the security of such sensitive areas as the USAREUR headquarters in Heidelberg, Germany – pursue an almost daily ritual of searching for light-hearted amusement. In this twisted environment of dark humor, they might turn on the electric current while a compatriot was repairing a light switch, just to watch him twerk.

As talented, dedicated, and duty-bound were the men of the 529th under normal circumstances during the decade of the '70s, there were also simply a number of "characters" there who were overly adept at ridiculous foolishness – sometimes to the detriment of their own safety.

### Not The Sharpest Knife

The late I.Q. Deficient (not his real name of course) was one such unusual soul. Blessed with movie-star good looks – great hair, an ever-present bright smile, broad shoulders and naturally muscular physique – I.Q. also had a gift for gab that just wouldn't quit. Women drooled over him.

According to his story, I.Q. had washed out of Airborne Infantry School due to "bad knees," and had somehow wound up in the 529th. I don't know if I believe that or not, but that was his story, and he stuck to it during his short time with the Deuce-Nine. Our unit was unique in that regard. It simply wasn't unusual for guys from unlikely places to appear within our ranks. The 529th, however, only retained the best. If one had flaws, he or she usually was eventually "weeded out."

By and large in the early 1970s, G.I.s had a difficult, at best, time acquiring female companionship, particularly that of an attractive German fraulein. These ladies, in general, simply snubbed most G.I.s. I guess "turn-about is fair play." After all, it had been barely 25 years or so since these G.I.s's fathers had subdued and imprisoned many of these "ladies'" fathers and grandfathers – some for "Crimes Against Humanity." So I suppose a little animosity was to be understood.

The mistake Americans seem to make time and time again, however, is the expenditure of the treasure of our country and the blood of our men to conquer an evil rogue empire, only to turn right around and not only give the country back to those rogues, but to spend our treasure yet again to *re-build* their devastated country. The logic defeats me... but I digress...

When it came to attracting German fraulein companionship, I.Q. Deficient just seemed to be an exception to the rule... and was a "natural" at the art. He always had an attractive German lady and it just didn't seem fair, because, to put it bluntly, despite all his admirable qualities, even I.Q. knew that he wasn't "the sharpest knife in the drawer."

Specialist Deficient also was forever bringing his female companionship into the barracks late at night, and forcing

*At least a portion of I.Q.'s popularity within the ranks of the 529th stemmed from the fact that he never knew an enemy or a stranger.*

the rookie G.I.s to listen to those ladies cooing and moaning in delight in the dark corner where he bunked. The fact that females were strictly forbidden in the barracks in the evenings was beside the point as far as I.Q. was concerned. The rules more often than not simply did not apply to him as far as he was concerned.

At least a portion of I.Q.'s popularity within the ranks of the 529th stemmed from the fact that he never knew an enemy or a stranger. That big smile rarely left his face and he incessantly circulated among all the troops, never favoring anyone and befriending almost everyone.

I.Q. often drew duty on the front gate at Patton Barracks. Pulling security on the gates was not the most inspirational or rewarding of jobs, and due to the drudgery of that task and Specialist Deficient's nevertheless happy-go-lucky nature, he was constantly in pursuit of the previously-explained amusements to pass the time.

One of I.Q.'s most favorite "diversions" was right around the corner from the Patton Barracks front gate at a little Italian restaurant called San Remo *(The restaurant and even the building have sadly disappeared completely from the landscape since the departure of US-AREUR from Heidelberg in 2013).* At the time, San Remo had some of the best cold beer in town. *(Though they were probably brewing it in an old car radiator out back...)*

This was the thing about the Patton gate gig. It offered several "options,"

The favorite haunt of "I.Q. Deficient" during his gate-guard duty at Patton Barracks was photographed in 1974. (Photo by Bob Walls)

if you will, to the enlisted men manning that post that the other duty stations couldn't provide. It therefore was I.Q.'s favorite post.

First of all, it offered "the San Remo boogey." No other 529th MP duty station had a restaurant with delightfully-cold German beer a mere 50 feet away. There simply were no "San Remos" (or any other such distraction) anywhere near any of the other duty-posts. All of the MPs at those sites were isolated in their work.

The Patton post also sometimes included a "non-NCO" (read Spec-4 rank) as the "desk sergeant," so this opened up the possibility of even more foolishness at this duty-post. This isn't to say that the Spec-4s assigned as desk sergeant there were unqualified or derelict in their duty. Not by a long shot. It's just that they sometimes didn't run quite as "tight a ship" as a hard NCO would have run, because they had to live with the men they were supervising, and "hard-case" Spec-4 desk sergeants had a tendency to be ostracized by the EMs. *(That obviously is the very reason that NCOs who live in the barracks invariably are isolated from the enlisted men.)*

The desk sergeant on duty at the

Patton gate also simply took it for granted that no one would ever be so brazen as to pull a San Remo beer-a-thon while on duty – that is, until I.Q. hit town. Things such as that just didn't happen in the 529th, but then again, as detailed above, I.Q. also was just a different breed of cat. He "dared to go where others feared to tread" – or something like that.

As a result of all of the above, I.Q. Deficient – on his fateful final day of duty in the 529th – was slipping back and forth – undeterred – to San Remo during his Patton gate-guard duty breaks. By 2:00 or 3:00 pm that afternoon, though he was still able to manage his gate-guard duty, Specialist Deficient should have been relieved from duty – mainly because he was "snockered" – not "hammered" – but snockered nonetheless. And I'm sure he would have been removed from duty if anyone had been aware of his shenanigans – but there simply wasn't any rule against taking one's hourly breaks in the cool inviting confines of San Remo, and who knew what he was doing while he was over there. Right?

Now in his "de-natured" condition and while standing in the traffic intersection supposedly checking identifications and controlling the traffic into Patton on a lazy summer Sunday afternoon when traffic was virtually nonexistent, I.Q. had dangerously decided he was going to practice "quick-jack-a-round-into-the-chamber" of his Colt .45 sidearm. *(A perfectly good example of the reason inebriated soldiers normally are immediately removed from duty and disciplined – but, again, I.Q. was an exception to the rule.)*

Somewhere along the line, someone had demonstrated to I.Q. that if he grasped the heavy .45 sidearm and pulled it partially up out of the holster and then – pressing it firmly (friction-wise) against the front of the holster – jammed the weapon back down inside the holster, he could jack a round into the chamber with only one hand.

I don't know the name of the M.P. who demonstrated this little foolishness to I.Q., but he should have been disciplined as well. I.Q. nevertheless, had actually become quite adept at this piece of dangerous showmanship and was understandably proud of his achievement.

As the hours passed and I.Q. went back and forth from San Remo to his gate guard gig, he continued practicing. He'd jack a round then look up and smile... Jack a round, look up and smile. *(And after each sequence, he was having to drop the .45's magazine, eject the live round, and then re-load it back into the magazine. In each instance, that round kept getting more and more difficult to load back into that magazine, and it eventually became comical to watch, as did much of I.Q.'s other actions at this point. Meanwhile, no one of a supervisory capacity had yet noticed or realized what was going on.)*

With something this dangerous, I.Q. Deficient's luck was bound to run out – and it eventually did. During one of his practices, his index finger apparently inevitably curled inside the trigger guard, causing him to accidentally pull the trigger as he jammed the weapon back down into his holster. *(Note: In case you, the readers, are wondering, I was off-duty on this day. I observed some of the above for a short period of time from*

> *As a tourniquet was being applied to his leg, EMTs attended to I.Q. until he could be loaded onto a gurney.*

*the second floor window on the north end of the Deuce-Nine barracks, but wasn't really aware of what I.Q. was doing until the hammer actually fell on this little incident. I was provided with the rest of the details from I.Q.'s gate-guard partner later-on that afternoon after all the excitement had died down.)*

One can only imagine Mr. Deficient's unmitigated shock when a huge resounding "boom" suddenly filled the courtyard area at the Patton gate. Timed almost perfectly with the discharge was a substantial hop I.Q. almost comically and spasmodically performed in his shocked reflexive response to the big .45's discharge. *(I did observe this portion of the incident.)*

Looking down quickly, I.Q. suddenly grasped the fact that blood was spurting out of his leg. The heavy .45 slug had entered his upper thigh, and, almost inexplicably, had traveled down through his knee – blowing it out – and then had exited from his lower leg. It's a substantial miracle that the round did not sever his femoral artery and bring about almost certain sudden death.

After he realized what had happened, I.Q. immediately hit the ground and began drawing quite a bit of attention. Troops began running to his aid and EMTs were quickly summoned. As a tourniquet was being applied to his leg, EMTs attended to I.Q. until he could be loaded onto a gurney.

A short time later as the EMTs carried him to the ambulance, I.Q. began going into shock. He started screaming at the top of his lungs – *"I'm off the gates! I'm off the gates! I'm off the gates forever! Ah ha! Ha! Ha!"*

And you know what? As things turned out, I.Q. was right.

After they had loaded him into the ambulance that day and driven away, I never again saw nor heard from I.Q. Deficient. He simply vanished from the public record, and faded into history.

Knowing him, he probably was honorably discharged, awarded a *Purple Heart* and *Good Conduct Medal*, and lived the remainder of his life on a fat monthly medical disability check, but that's just this present-day layman's assessment.

Later that same day, it was decided that the round which had passed through I.Q.'s leg needed to be located. I suspect this was desired for the incident report. I went down to help search, and won the lottery when, approximately 100 feet from where I.Q. had been standing, I discovered the still-bloody slug on the cobblestones in the street. It apparently had exited I.Q.'s leg, bounced skyward off the cobblestones, and then fallen back onto the ground.

A number of years later, when a roster of the 529th Military Police Company veterans began circulating, I noticed that the ever-colorful I.Q. Deficient unfortunately was listed as "deceased." As sad as was that discovery, I have to admit it didn't surprise me.

I salute your eternal happiness and always effervescent personality I.Q. You will be long remembered.

### Gene's Latrine

During the early days of my assignment to the 529th, I often drew duty providing security at the CINC's home in the hills above Heidelberg. This home – or estate – had obviously belonged to someone of substantial wealth prior to the American takeover in Germany, and it apparently was a great place for dinner parties, because VIPs were hosted there regularly.

Though duty at the CINC's residence was yet another somewhat tedious and dull security task, it was at least refreshing to be able to walk around in the cool mountain air and patrol the substantial grounds which were heavily planted with towering trees and beautiful flowering shrubs in the well-manicured lawn. There was a long winding trail around the perimeter and up through the hills of the four- or five-acre estate.

Though the work was mentally numbing, we were very cautious and meticulous nonetheless regarding this duty. Looking back, it is very fortunate that we were too, because some dangerous people apparently were watching us. *(More about that later.)*

This was all well and good in the spring, summer, and autumn, but when winter set in, it could get bitterly cold up there in the mountains. This occasionally included substantial snowfall too.

Yet another of the "characters" in the 529th was easy-going "Good-Time Gene" (obviously not his real name either). Gene just rarely got upset about anything, no matter the nature of the beast – but he did regularly deal with the boredom problem through which we all suffered.

In November of 1972, according to a letter I wrote home at the time, I drew duty as an usher at a special dinner at Gen. Davison's home. He was hosting Gen. Creighton W. Abrams among other dignitaries. Good-Time Gene was one of the Deuce-Niners assigned as security at the general's mansion that evening.

Gene was a draftee much like

many of the guys in the 529th. He was just marking time until he could return home and help his dad with the family business back in Miami.

On this evening while Gene was patrolling the CINC's estate during the dinner party for the aforementioned dignitaries, he apparently decided to seek a distraction. There was a broad beautifully-landscaped expanse of open hillside which was viewable from a large picture-window in the dining area inside the CINC's residence. Perhaps Gene was unaware of this. I don't know.

There had been a significant snowfall the previous day – perhaps 12 to 14 inches. I mean it was deep and it was cold as afternoon receded into evening.

In his patrolling boredom, Gene left the CINC gate-shack, slung his M-16 onto his shoulder, and marched out to the broad hillside meadow openly viewable from the General's elegant dining area. He began idly tramping in the snow. It almost looked like he was creating a big latrine in the white stuff until one got far enough away to be able to visualize the object of Good-Time's attentions.

What Gene had actually been producing was large 20-foot letters which spelled "FTA." Now virtually anyone in that day and time – including the General and most of his guests no doubt – knew that "FTA" was an acronym for "F___ the Army." At that time, due to the debacle in Vietnam, the U.S. Army was suffering through a terrible image problem and epithets such as FTA were widely used to disparage it and anything connected with it.

As a result, "FTA" obviously was not something one wants to inscribe upon a four-star general's front lawn – especially where it is in full view of his dignified military guests as well.

Needless to say, the CINC – who was also the Army Commander of NATO – was not amused with Gene's little note to his guests.

I don't know what prompted Gene to create such a blatant insult to a four-star general who had dedicated his life to a career in the military. Perhaps Gene somehow thought that he was invisible – or perhaps that he was invulnerable to punishment.

I don't recall the nature of Gene's ultimate punishment for this transgression either, but I'm certain he didn't walk away from it without some type of training reformation. Knowing "Good-Time Gene," though, it probably was of little concern no matter how harsh.

### Spec-4 Justin A. Hole

Another of the incidents which went down in the lore of the 529th for a number of years occurred one evening at one of the favorite watering holes of Deuce-Niners in downtown Heidelberg. It quite possibly would never have occurred without the influence of German beer. No.... Actually, that's just not true. I'm sure it would inevitably have occurred regardless of the circumstances.

Zillertal's was a small bar and pub near the historic Hauptstrasse (main street of old-town Heidelberg) which had been patronized consistently by the troops of the 529th for a decade or more prior to the early 1970s. It fell out of favor sometime in the mid- to late-1970s with the advent of the discos and other more-popular clubs such as "Shepherd's" downtown, but for awhile, "Zill's" was riding high – literally. I'm certain it is long-gone today.

At any rate, on a warm summer evening in 1974, a group of us had gathered there as we occasionally still did. One of the guys who participated on this evening – we'll call him "Justin A. Hole" – was your proto-typical bully, who enjoyed humiliating others for reasons I still don't understand. I mean this guy was blessed with good looks and intelligence and a great job within the Deuce-Nine, yet spent untold hours constantly abusing the enlisted men.

As stated, Spec-4 Hole had a cushy job on the administrative side of the 529th, and, as such, was never exposed to the rigors, boredom, - and, yes, even dangers – of "gate-guard" duty. In fact, he was never required to pull any M.P. duty at all, and, in general, just lived "the life of Riley." He was another of those who were simply blessed with good fortune and widely envied by the line troops. Despite all his blessings, though, it was just never enough for this guy.

On this night at Zillertals, Specialist Hole was more abusive than normal (if that was even possible). The guy he had targeted for abuse that evening – we'll call him "Bill," – was relatively new in the 529th and unaware of Hole's penchant for doling out abuse.

The further Mr. Hole got into his mugs of beer, the more abusive he became too. Bill was one of Hole's typical victims. He was somewhat reserved; intelligent; and a pretty sharp dude overall, and Hole was just naturally antagonistic to those types. And the longer Bill simply good-naturedly endured Hole's torment, the nastier Spec-4 Justin A. Hole became.

Yet another guy in our group – Sgt. Ewer Dirtnap – (Nah…not his name

*And the longer Bill simply good-naturedly endured Hole's torment, the nastier Spec-4 Justin A. Hole became.*

either of course.) was a beefy, ham-fisted, happy-go-lucky guy from the Mid-West. Virtually everyone liked Ewer. He was the polar-opposite of Justin A. Hole – always with a wide friendly smile, just like a big friendly puppy.

As the evening wore on, Hole's taunts eventually began taking a toll on Bill, and most everyone in the group sympathized with him. After listening to Hole's mouth for an hour or two, many of us – Sgt. Dirtnap in particular – truly wanted to shut him up.

Finally, totally exasperated, Bill got up to leave when he could tolerate Hole's insults no longer. Sgt. Dirtnap, with a heart the size of Manhattan and the courage of a lion, stopped the young man and calmly said, "Hang on. Don't leave. Let me handle this. Exchange seats with me."

When this happened, we all just thought that Ewer was going to pull Hole aside and give him a good tongue-lashing. News flash… That wasn't even a consideration for Sgt. Dirtnap.

To the eternal appreciation of those of us present, Ewer didn't waste any time whatsoever with words. Specialist Hole was still yammering on incessantly when the good sergeant drew that big ham-fisted right arm of his wayyyyyy back – oh, I'd say back down somewhere around Africa – and when it shot forward like a howitzer round, it caught Hole flush on the left eye with a punch his great-great-grandfather felt. And when Hole stood up quickly to engage Ewer, Dirtnap delivered one of the most memorable left upper-cuts I have ever seen. It would have brought a smile even to the face of Mike Tyson. It sent Hole ass over elbows backwards out of his chair and onto the floor.

Sgt. Dirtnap wasn't done yet either. He calmly rose from his seat at the table and walked around to stand over the prostrate Hole (who by then was waving away the stars floating around his head) and got right down in his face and said, "If you ever open your mouth to abuse anyone in this unit like that ever again, I'll give you double what you just got. You hear me soldier??!!"

I don't know if Specialist Justin A. Hole actually heard Ewer or not. He was still shaking out the cobwebs and trying to figure out where he was. After a few moments, he recovered a bit and, without a word, got up and staggered off, back to the barracks.

The next morning – whoa baby! – it was "shiner city" for Hole. The entire area around and within his left eye socket was dark black, blue and bloody, and remained that way for well over a week. And, to the surprise of many, Justin had suddenly become a walking road-sign for humility too.

From that point forward, every time he was about to meet someone from our group on the street or in a hallway or anywhere else, Hole immediately turned and walked in another direction. His abusive nature had evaporated, and his personality had changed 180 degrees – literally. Sgt. Ewer Dirtnap had gotten his attention big-time.

I'll never forget Dirtnap's big smiling face and one resoundingly impressive night at Zillertal's way back in 1974, when he entered the folklore of the Deuce-Nine.

## Stan and the English Chicks

One of the truly amazing mysteries of life is the almost magical and many times inexplicable attraction of a particular female to a particular male. What one female finds attractive in a male may be truly repugnant to another of the feminine sex. I learned early-on that there simply is no rhyme or reason to this often paradoxical situation. It sometimes is just beyond explanation.

I was exposed to a particularly impressive example of this while in the 529th in 1973. Several of us had dropped by on our day off at an apartment rented by Stan K. Fingers *(Nope. Not his real name either.)* and several other Deuce-Niners. We often got together to play poker and pass the hours.

Now Stan was not one of the line-MPs at the 529th. To the contrary, he was a mechanic who worked in the motor pool, keeping our Jeeps, patrol sedans, and three-quarter-ton vehicles, etc. serviced and in good running condition.

Specialist Fingers was another of those guys who was popular around the company almost from Day 1. He was friendly to a fault and usually very conversational, invariably with some humorous story to relate. He also was another one who always seemed to have a smile on his face and a song in his heart. *(Funny how those attributes always win friends, huh?)*

Now due simply to the nature of his job, Stan almost always had a sloppy uniform, scuffed-up, un-shined, oil-soaked boots, and, more often than not, just a generally "greasy" unkempt appearance – inevitably with dark caked grease beneath his fingernails. *(Hey. . . It's simply the mechanic's persona. Always has been and always will be.)*

To put it bluntly, Stan K. Fingers had motor oil running through his veins.

Automotive mechanical work was his life. If he'd had manicured nails, a neat hair-cut, and tidy neat clothing, we very definitely would have wondered about him in the opposite direction... Ya know??

Anyway, despite his unattractive features, Stan – just like I.Q. (see above) – was surprisingly popular among the ladies. Also as explained above, in the early days when most American G.I.s were getting snubbed by the German ladies, Mr. Fingers – grubby fingernails, greasy uniform and all – invariably was stylin' with a foxy lady in tow. Sometimes the breath-taking quality of these ladies shocked us too.

One incident in particular involving Stan K. stands out in my memory – that of "the English chicks."

Heidelberg quite often was frequented by attractive females from "across the pond" in England. At that time, our historic little burg was a popular and inexpensive tourism destination for the British ladies. It also attracted the females because it had two major sites of higher learning – Schiller College and the University of Heidelberg. For whatever reason, there frequently were attractive ladies from the United Kingdom for our viewing pleasure, but just like all the other females, they almost invariably were simply "out of reach" for GIs.

On one particular occasion, I have to admit I was stunned to discover that Stan had not "one," but "two" of these ladies, and not only was he sporting them around town, they had even decided to take up temporary residence at his

*At that time, our historic little burg was a popular and inexpensive tourism destination for the British ladies.*

apartment. And these females weren't just attractive... Sports fans, these ladies were "drop-dead gorgeous." I simply couldn't believe it. How did he do it?

Stan never attempted to do a thing about his appearance for these ladies either yet they seemed to be absolutely crazy about him. And when I say "crazy," I mean "sex-thang" crazy. Stan K. Fingers had it going on...

On the morning that we had dropped by his apartment, we had done so just to snag a bit of exposure to these gorgeous "ladies." One of Stan K.'s roommates who also worked in the motor pool – and who shall remain nameless – was sitting at the kitchen table on this morning wolfing down some warm buttered toast with jelly when we came rolling in. (*He didn't offer us any of the toast, gobbling it down himself. We, however, shortly were greatly relieved that he hadn't.*)

Stan soon joined us from the bedroom, explaining the "ladies" were still "sleeping it off" from the previous night's festivities downtown. "Yeah, we got up for a little while early this morning to eat some breakfast," he snorted, chest puffed out... "but then couldn't resist a little wild stuff on the kitchen table, ya know. Used the butter-stick on 'em," he added with a wolfish grin on his face, nodding toward the now mostly-depleted stick of margarine his roommate had been scarfing down.

Those words had scarcely left Stan's mouth before his roommate began choking and sputtering, hopping over to the kitchen sink to croak up his buttered toast. When he had recovered, he turned red-faced to Stan, steam shooting from his ears, and bellowed "You did whattttt!!!!????"

At this point, Specialist Fingers – immensely enjoying the mounting humor in this situation – was overcome with mirth. "Yeah!" he croaked... "Both of 'em!"

"I'll kill you" his roommate bellowed, lunging at Stan who by that point had quickly retreated back into the bedroom where he had slammed and locked the door behind him, breathless from laughter.

"Absolutely amazing," was all we could say or think as we left that day. Yep... Stan K. Fingers had it going on.... And none of us could eat hot buttered toast for awhile.

### Big Bad Ed

I don't remember exactly when I first became aware of Ed Meek's presence in the Deuce-Nine, but it must have been sometime around mid-April of 1972 shortly after I arrived at the 529th. *(It was difficult to miss him in all honesty...)*

At that time, Ed was an "upper-classman" in the 529th, along with the likes of Barry Willis, Donald "Dutch" Wierzema, "Penny" Harrington, John "Thumper" Thornton, Tony Mosca, Les Toon, Jim Hewitt, and others. Ed was one of those people who just seemed to have a "presence" among his peers.

I think he was aware of this too. He sometimes wore one of those "flapjack hats." You know... those tough-guy "Jersey" hats. The one that the cigar-chomping ex-boxer down on the waterfront wore when he waded into a bar. What most people didn't know was that Ed Meek actually was anything but

Ed Meek, pictured here in 1973 at a company cook-out in the rear "social area" of Building 103, was a member of the USAREUR "Color Guard" detachment.

confrontational – but he rarely if ever let anyone know it. It would've wrecked his "street cred."

Anyway, the days and months rolled on, and I eventually got to know Ed simply through our work as MPs, and because he associated with one or two of the guys with whom I hung. About a year after I arrived, Ed had moved to an apartment off-post out in the nearby community of Nussloch with John Thornton, Dudley Webb and one or two other guys. When John's tour of duty expired and he departed Heidelberg, Ed asked if I was interested in moving into John's old room and helping them pay the rent. I said "Sure."

After a few weeks, as GIs in Heidelberg almost invariably did, we – in our constant pursuit of female companionship – began making regular trips down to the bars along the Hauptstrasse in the old-town section of the city. Eventually it got around to going in groups of threes and fours down to Zillertal's or Shepherd's or one of the other clubs or bars. Sometimes we'd go out to the riverside parks and play football and admire the ladies longingly out there.

Contrary to some other folks, Meek was one of those guys who never became abrasive or obnoxious after a few beers either. To the contrary, he simply became amusing – and a little more vocal. Occasionally, he was downright hilarious. And that was all well and good as long as things cruised along smoothly, but if someone became obnoxious or offensive to him – lookout. The ride was about to get bumpy.

Anyway, on one of these occasions – in which I was not present to the best of my knowledge – Meek related to me one incident which occurred. He explained that he and several buddies were hanging out downtown at "Shepherds," when they decided to try another bar.

Now one has to understand, that in those days (1972-1974), contrary to what many people thought, Germany wasn't exactly a "walk in the park." Terrorist bombings at U.S.

*Contrary to some other folks, Meek was one of those guys who never became abrasive or obnoxious after a few beers either.*

*He explained that he and several buddies were hanging out downtown at "Shepherds," when they decided to try another bar.*

military installations were becoming commonplace, occurring several times a month – and people were dying. To say the least, it was just a hair on the dangerous side, particularly for MPs. Nothing terribly excessive, but enough to often keep MPs on the jumpy side. One never knew when, as a security guard at one of the many sites patrolled by the 529th, a vehicle was going to roll up loaded with explosives and rearrange a city block, just as happened on May 24, 1974 at Campbell Barracks where the 529th secured the premises.

As a result, most MPs of that day had somewhat of an "edge" to them. And they therefore sometimes just needed an opportunity to blow off some steam; it was only natural. The ways we did that were many and varied, and, for the most part, are better left undisclosed and forgotten.

"I remember leaving Shepherds that day with a couple of MPs that I hung with," Meek explained matter-of-factly. "We'd been enjoying that great German beer. One of these guys suddenly picked up a street sign which still had the heavy cement anchor attached to it, and literally tossed it through the back window of a nearby car. And I'm thinking to myself... 'Did he really just do that?' I not only was shocked, I was pretty bent about it to be honest. There was no call for that."

Meek continued by explaining that one thing led to another, and before they knew it, one of the guys had confronted the other about what had just transpired, and the fisticuffs began to fly. "Someone apparently called the German Police (Polizei)," he added. "We didn't want to get run in for *'Drunk & Disorderly'* and *'Destruction of Property,'"* he laughed. "First of all, we **were** the police and were supposed to be setting an example for good behavior, and secondly, we knew that if word of this little incident got back to the First Sergeant, there was going to be Hell to pay, and who needs that? So what did we do? Well... For starters, we ran! – just like common criminals!" he laughed.

Meek apparently was swifter afoot than his buddies, because the Polizei caught them, but not Mercury Meek from Ohio. "I felt guilty about running off on them though, so I turned around and went back" he smiled in remembrance, "and we actually talked our way out of it eventually, but not out of the damage report which apparently had been turned in by the Polizei.

"The next day at Guard-Mount, one of the guys had a huge black eye, and I asked him what had happened. He said

*"Long story short, the First Sergeant, surprisingly, was cool about the situation after we talked it out," Meek added.*

'During the melee, you slugged me you damn idiot!' Ooooppss."

Worse yet, Army CID (Criminal Investigation Division) had gotten wind of the incident, so Meek and his cronies now had to "pay the piper" with them. "I was called to the Orderly Office," he continued. "My 'buddy' – the guy with the black eye – had apparently filed a complaint against me! It stated that I not only had assaulted him, but that I had also broken an expensive watch he was wearing.

"Long story short, the First Sergeant, surprisingly, was cool about the situation after we talked it out," Meek added. "I'm sure they realized there wasn't any reason to get into any big charges or punishment for a little incident like this. They said that if I paid for the guy's watch (and the broken car window), I wouldn't be charged with anything."

All of which was fortunate for Ed Meek. He had a Top Secret (TS) security clearance and often worked at the CINC's offices in the Command Building – a cushy job that I'm certain he didn't want to jeopardize. Those TS clearances didn't come cheap either.

But that was Ed Meek – as his "buddy" had discovered. If you were going to "cross him," you better take him down and end it quick, cause he was a "gamer." (Probably still is.)

*"My 'buddy' – the guy with the black eye – had apparently filed a complaint against me!"*

## Chapter 10

*≈*

# Protecting the CINC of the U.S. Army in Europe

In the decade of the 1970s, slightly more than 270,000 American Army troops were stationed in Europe at any given time. These men and the installations and equipment they maintained, were all commanded by Gen. Michael S. Davison, Commander-in-Chief of the United States Army in Europe (USAREUR). The defense and protection of Gen. Davison and his staff were provided solely by the 529th Military Police Company in Heidelberg.

Though some 32 acts of terrorism occurred at U.S. military installations in Germany in 1970 alone, these, for the most part, consisted of attacks upon unguarded locales. Inexperienced terrorists were striking soft targets only, but that would all soon change. A much more determined, well-trained, and better-armed group of vigilantes – many of whom were the children of former Nazi military personnel in Germany – had made it their personal

*In the decade of the 1970s, slightly more than 270,000 American Army troops were stationed in Europe at any given time.*

mission in life to oust the American presence in Europe – and they were deadly-serious. U.S. soldiers shortly began losing their lives.

General Davison – who had seen duty in a number of different theatres of war by the time he was named CINC-Europe – had obviously been under fire in his military career. Twice-wounded in action in World War II, he was highly-decorated – a Silver Star recipient among other awards – long before he assumed command of the troops in Europe.

During the decade of the 1970s (and indeed from the 1960s to 2012), troops from the 529th Military Police Company were assigned to provide security at the USAREUR headquarters building, the facilities at Campbell and Patton Barracks, and much more around the clock, 24-7, 365 days a year in Heidelberg. This security presence was also provided for the CINC's residence and his family.

The CINC's

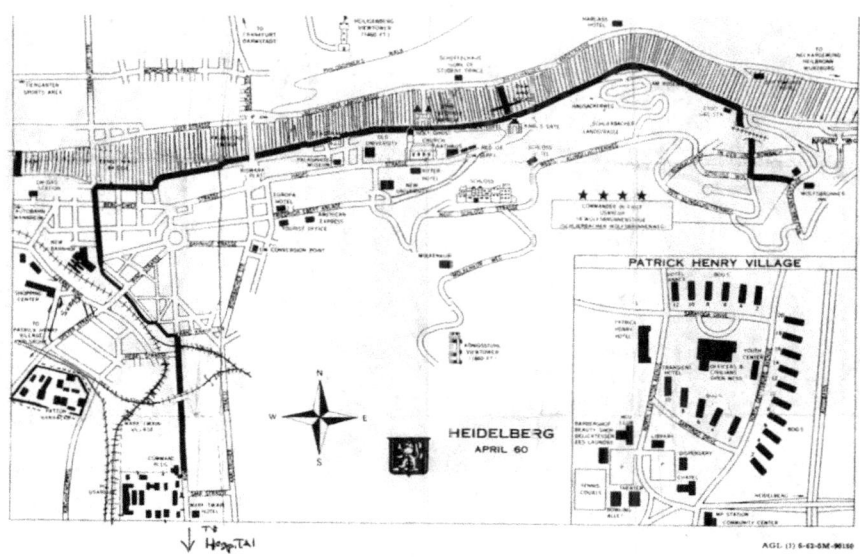

The route the CINC traveled each day to the Command Building (later re-named "the Keyes Building") from his home is outlined on this map. Terrorists were never able to focus upon Gen. Davison directly, but his successor was attacked on this route by a determined group with rocket-propelled grenades and automatic weapons, very nearly assassinating him. Though the attackers on that day were successful in striking the CINC's vehicle, the additional armor plating protected him from fatal injury, though he did suffer wounds from the incident.

estate was approximately three to five acres in size and had a winding trail around the periphery of the property. It was somewhat isolated, and could possibly have been problematic – at least in the short term – had a concerted effort ever been mounted by determined aggressors to assault it, but no such assault ever occurred – at least not during the decade of the 1970s.

This detail at the CINC's residence included a non-commissioned-officer-in-charge (NCOIC) and two to four security guards – depending upon the circumstances. A heated gate shack provided a measure of comfort when the cold winter weather arrived, and it was cool up in the mountains at the residence in the summertime, so it wasn't bad duty most of the time.

The front gate, which was the only entrance into the residence, was heavily-guarded, and regular patrols were made around the perimeter of the estate. The MPs on duty were always armed with Colt .45 side-arms and M-16s for these security missions.

Quite often in the mornings during the spring, summer and autumn, General Davison liked to go jogging on the mountain roads above his residence. When this occurred, the two MPs guarding the front gate would routinely be facing toward the outside of the gate, cautiously observing any vehicular traffic and/or pedestrians in the area, when they would suddenly be surprised by Gen. Davison's presence behind them.

On one occasion, I will never forget my surprise as he jogged out the front

The residence of the commander-in-chief of the United States Army in Europe (and also the Army Commander of NATO) Gen. Michael S. Davison, photographed in 1974. The 529th Military Police Company was charged with the constant security of Gen. Davison. The 529th MP Guard Shack is visible inside the gate on the right. (Photo by R.O. Jackson)

gate, bidding us "Good morning." Carrying a fully-loaded M-16 carbine and a holstered Colt .45, I immediately began jogging protectively behind him. The task of running in full gear wasn't that unusual, since we were only a few months removed from the toughness of Basic Training, but I have to admit I absolutely was not looking forward to it that day. Not only was the gear heavy, the day was very hot, and those mountain roads were very steep.

When he noticed I was following him from a distance, the general – to my undying appreciation – motioned to me to stop and return to my post. Despite the fact that he was a four-star, my duty was unequivocal – to protect him at all costs – so I politely ignored his directives and continued following behind him.

When the general realized I was still with him, he paused, telling me he was grateful for the protection, but explained that he would become that much more of a target if anyone noticed he was being followed by a heavily-armed military policeman. "Please just return to your post and I'll be back in a few minutes," he said.

At that point, having just received a direct instruction from him, I wasn't about to disobey a four-star general, so I gladly returned to the Gate Guard Shack at the entrance to his residence.

As stated above, no one ever penetrated the protection provided to the CINC on our watch, but a new CINC approximately nine years later would not be so fortunate. *(Readers please see "Terrorist Attack of 1981" in this volume.)*

# Chapter 11

# The USAREUR Color Guard

O ne of the few "plum assign-ments" at the 529th MP Com-pany was membership on the USAREUR "Color Guard." This pres-tigious unit represented the USAREUR command, posting the colors and serv-ing in official ceremonies and goodwill capacities throughout Europe. Selection for this detail meant you were consid-ered to be one of the best representatives available for the U.S. Army in Europe.

To qualify for the Color Guard, one had to have consistently demon-strated mature judgement, firm guid-ance, strong leadership qualities, an un-blemished military record, and a strong respect for national symbols such as the

American flag. One also had to have demonstrated a sense of knowledge and ability beyond that of the average sol-dier, and to have presented consistent-ly-impressive military appearance, pres-ence and attention to detail which also excelled beyond that of the average sol-dier. Physically, one was required to be at least 6 feet tall, trim and in excellent physical condition, and to have served capably and honorably as a military po-liceman for a period of time acceptable to those judging the selections for Col-or Guard duty.

One of the best aspects of being se-lected for the USAREUR Color Guard was that it provided an entre' to the best of all the posts available among the men of the 529th. Those included the

The 1972 USAREUR Color Guard was photo-graphed here with two members of the German Army Color Guard. Pictured (L-R) are Spec-4 Randy Roberts, right rifleman; Spec-4 Kyle Harris, flag-bearer; German Army unknown; German Army unknown; Sgt. Frank Withers, flag-bearer; Spec-4 Ed Meek, flag-bearer; and Spec-4 Donald "Dutch" Wiersema, left ri-fleman. This photo was taken during a cere-mony at the USAREUR Command Building on Romerstrasse.

The 1973 USAREUR Color Guard were (L-R) Spec-4 R.O. Jackson, right rifleman; Sgt. Ran-dy Roberts, flag-bearer; Spec-4 Kyle Harris, flag-bearer; Spec-4 Jack Williams, flag-bear-er; and Spec-4 Donald "Dutch" Wiersema, left rifleman.

The USAREUR Color Guard steps out in a ceremony at the Campbell Barracks parade ground with a modern contingent of the German Army. Pictured in this 1974 version of the Guard are (R-L) Spec-4 R.O. Jackson, left rifleman; Spec-4 Jack Williams, flag-bearer; Spec-4 Terry Brocksmith, flag-bearer; SSG Patrick R. Mackay, flag-bearer; and Spec-4 Daniel Norman, right rifleman.

Absolute precision was demanded of those who earned appointment to the Color Guard detail. As good as the perfection appears in this photo, it would not be acceptable once reviewed, and would later require more practice by those involved. Pictured here (L-R) are: Spec-4 Donald "Dutch" Wiersema, left rifleman; Spec-4 Jack Williams, flag-bearer; Spec-4 Kyle Harris, flag-bearer; Sgt. Randy Roberts, flag-bearer; and Spec-4 R.O. Jackson, right rifleman.

Each year in the early 1970s, the 529th Military Police "Color Guard" in representation of the United States Army in Europe traveled to famed Lourdes, France, high in the Pyrenees for a highly popular religious pilgrimage.

A portion of each ceremonial Honor Guard event invariably involved a dramatic cannon salute. One of the large 105 mm guns is manned here in the early 1970s by Spec-4 Bob "Wally" Walls (facing camera) and another unidentified individual.

USAREUR Command Building; service as an M.P. duty desk sergeant at either Patton or Campbell Barracks; service in the administrative offices of the 529th; and service as a duty-driver of the Jeeps and 529th Patrol Cruisers shuttling men to the various 529th duty stations.

These assignments meant that one's days freezing and/or standing in the rain on gate-guard duty at Campbell or Patton Barracks, or security guard duty at the CINC's aircraft at the USAREUR Air Strip, or security guard duty at the CINC's personal quarters had come to a close – usually.

Many members of the USAREUR Color Guard worked almost exclusively at the USAREUR Command Building, providing security for the CINC, his staff and offices. This was considered a top echelon duty-station in the 529th.

Duty at the Command Building, however, also meant one had to successfully pass an in-depth background check. The Command Building post required a Top Secret Security Clearance. It wasn't impossible for one to finally attain status as a member of the USAREUR Color Guard and then fail the background check. If and when that occurred, it was usually "Back to the gate-show you go."

The evolution of those assigned to the Color Guard from 1972 to 1975 was as follows:

In 1972, the Color Guard consisted of Spec-4 Randy "Oral" Roberts on right rifle; Spec-4 Kyle Harris as flag-bearer; Sgt. Frank Withers as flag-bearer; Spec-4 Ed Meek as flag-bearer; and Spec-4 Donald "Dutch" Wierzema as left rifle.

By late 1972 or early 1973, due to the departure of several of its members back to civilian life, the Color Guard consisted of Spec-4 R.O. Jackson on right rifle; Sgt. Randy "Oral" Roberts as flag-bearer; Spec-4 Kyle Harris as flag-bearer; Spec-4 Jack Williams as flag-bearer; and Spec-4 Donald "Dutch" Wierzema as left rifle.

In 1974, after several more members had ETSed (Expected Time of Separation) from the Army, the Color Guard consisted of Spec-4 R.O. Jackson as left rifle; SSG Patrick Mackay as flag-bearer; Spec-4 Terry Brocksmith as flag-bearer (alternating with Spec-4 Mark Watson); Spec-4 Jack Williams as flag-bearer; and Spec-4 Daniel Norman as right rifle.

Though it was a highly-desirable post, Color Guard duty required hours of marching practice and close-order drill. It also required additional intensive work on "polishing," "shining," "ironing," "starching," and "marching" far beyond that of the average soldier. In the USAREUR Color Guard, only the finest precision in all drills was acceptable.

# Chapter 12

# Command Building Duty

T he Command Building – more formally identified as "the Keyes Building" in 1974 – had been constructed in 1936-'37 as an officer's club and dining facility for officers in the Nazi 110th Grenadier (Infantry) Regiment which once was headquartered in Heidelberg at the Romerstrasse and Kircheimer Weg installations (later known respectively as Campbell and Patton Barracks). After being taken over by American forces in late 1945, the Nazi officers' club was re-designated as "the Command Building" of the United States Army in Europe (USAREUR) and assigned to the USAREUR commander and his staff.

The 529th Military Police (MP) Company was permanently charged with the responsibility of security not only for this building, but, as previously explained, the Campbell Barracks complex, Patton Barracks, the CINC's residence, the Deputy-CINC's residence, the "War Room" inside Campbell, and the aircraft and air-strip assigned to the CINC a short distance outside Heidelberg.

The 529th MPs assigned to the War Room (actually the command and control center for USAREUR in a time of war) were required to have the highest security clearances – "Secret Intelligence." Those assigned to the Command Building were required to have the next highest clearance – "Top Secret."

Daytime MP duty at the Command

Spec-4 R.O. Jackson on desk sergeant duty at the highly-sensitive Command Building housing the offices and staff of the Commander-in-Chief of the United States Army in Europe, Gen. Michael S. Davison. (Photo by Jim Beardwood)

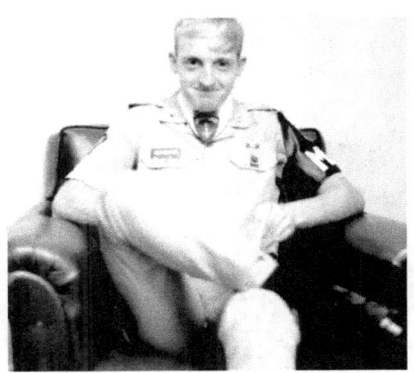

Spec-4 Jimmy Beardwood takes a break from desk-sergeant duties at the Command Building. Though he was never associated with the USAREUR "Color Guard," Beardwood had a permanent assignment to the Command Building detail (1973-1974), such was his attention to detail and responsibility.

Spec-4 Randy Duvall is unable to resist an opportunity to model the CINC's famed cavalry hat from his days as a commander in Vietnam.

Building was exceptionally serious business. General-grade officers came and went constantly and security inspections and checks were regularly required at specific times and places in the building; weapons had to be constantly maintained and in a ready status; and one had to be constantly attuned to any possible threats to the security of the building and/or the officers and staff therein. It was a cushy job to some degree – but it was also deadly serious business.

Evening MP duty at the Command Building, however, was a somewhat different story. Usually by 8:00 pm at the latest, all the staff had vacated the building. All entrances and access were shut down and locked. It became a totally-uneventful place and quiet as a tomb. Monotony set in with a flourish.

When I was assigned to the Command Building in 1973-74, I was told at that time that I was being cleared for a Top Secret. I never learned whether or not I ever received the clearance. This was at about the same time that America's Armed Forces pulled out of Vietnam, the debacle involving Nixon and

his resignation was occurring, and budgets were being slashed and reductions in forces were occurring throughout the American military infrastructure. I suspect an expensive and time-consuming clearance for a lowly Spec-4 in Heidelberg at that time simply wasn't very high on the Pentagon agenda.

On my shift, I usually worked with Spec-4 "Dutch" Wierzema, Spec-4 Ed Meek, Spec-4 Les Toon, Spec-4 Jimmy Beardwood, Spec-4 Mark Watson, Spec-4 Jack Williams, and several other rotating individuals. Assignment to the Command Building was usually a permanent detail, but could be altered occasionally for various and sundry reasons. I sometimes was assigned as desk sergeant at Patton and sometimes as a duty-driver of the MP Jeep and/or patrol unit as was Spec-4 Williams.

Due to the fact that "sleeping" understandably was absolutely forbidden on duty, the members of the 529th evening crew at the Command Building could often get creative in their duties and "endeavors" when the big building was silent and devoid of staff. Early one morning, around 2:00 or 3:00 am, one such incident got the attention of a number of people in a big way.

I also have to explain at this point that, due to the fact that the Command Building was such a highly-sensitive site at which Top Secret information flowed back and forth on a daily basis, a USAREUR "duty-officer" was always present and on duty in the evening hours inside the building in case some event tantamount to an emergency occurred in the European Theater of Operations.

In the early 1970s, the evening environment within the Command Building – as explained above – was dead-quiet, and the duty officer – usually someone of the rank of major or higher – was

Spec-4 Jimmy Beardwood (l) and Spec-4 R.O. Jackson take a moment to clown for the camera as they make their mid-night inspection rounds in the highly-sensitive USAREUR Command Building. (Photo by Bob Walls)

required to be present. This duty officer, interestingly, was also actually allowed to sleep in the duty office each evening if my memory serves me correctly.

Since the exceptional incident which I am about to describe occurred during the evening shift – and I came on-duty for the day-shift on this day several hours later – I received an explanation of this incident "second-hand," but the way it was explained to me was as follows:

The Deuce-Niner involved – who shall remain nameless – apparently was practicing his "quick-draw" down the hallway to the left as one entered the Command Building. During the period of the terrorist attacks in Germany in the 1970s, many of those on duty kept a round chambered in their Colt .45 sidearm – safety on. As John Wayne once

quipped, *"A gun that ain't loaded and ready ain't much use to the fast-draw in a gunfight."*

I don't know how the soldier on duty was able to do it, but he somehow quickly drew his weapon and accidentally fired it while practicing his quick-draw. I won't speculate any further. Suffice it to say that many of those on duty – particularly late at night – simply carried their weapons ready to fire at a moment's notice. Following the terrorist attack of May 24, 1972, which occurred 100 yards away in Campbell Barracks, circumstances were tense everywhere for 529th MPs for a number of months (as they were for all MPs throughout Germany where terrorist attacks were occurring several times a month."

This, apparently, was exactly the

With dilapidation and decay setting in, it is apparent from this photo that the historic Command Building - a center of power in the United States Army chain of command since 1945 - has, sadly, been abandoned by U.S. troops. This photo was snapped circa 2016 after this structure was returned to the ownership of the German government. The brass plaque identifying this structure as "the Keyes Building" remains mounted to the right of the doorway. Gen. Geoffrey Keyes was a prominent member of the staff of fabled Gen. George S. Patton during World War II.

situation on the morning in question at the Command Building. The individual – and again, he shall remain nameless – apparently had a round chambered when he quickly drew his weapon to practice his quick draw reflexes, and, as explained above, the weapon discharged.

The resulting deafening roar from the discharged round within the confined quarters of the Command Building hallway can only be imagined today, but one knows without question that it was loud – really loud.

The heavy .45 caliber round struck the wall beside the right door jamb of the entryway from the lobby into the left hallway containing the offices of the CINC's staff. The individual whose weapon had fired undoubtedly was shocked beyond description.

The most surprising aspect of this entire event, however, wasn't so much the firing of the round, but the fact that the duty officer – asleep within an office about halfway down the very hallway as that through which the round was fired – NEVER AWOKE, NOR EVER EVEN FILED A REPORT OF THE INCIDENT as far as I know. How one could sleep through such a horrendous noise is unknown.

Needless to say, when the NCOIC (non-commissioned officer in charge) who patrolled the 529th duty stations arrived at the Command Building that morning, he apparently was filled-in on the details. *(It, after all, was difficult to miss the big bullet hole and splintered wood in the doorjamb.)*

The NCOIC therefore obviously filed his report with the Commandant of Patton Barracks – Colonel Charles Shay – who also was the semi-top dawg in the 529th chain of command. Col. Shay – one of the most "no nonsense" yet reasonable officers I have ever known – apparently smoothed things over. Sometime later that day, I believe a workman quietly "puttied up" the hole in the door jamb and then deftly painted over it.

I'm sure the soldier committing the offence was severely reprimanded. Whether or not he ever again worked the Command Building is unknown by this writer.

Though events such as that above paint the 529th with a careless and callous brush, nothing could actually be further from the truth. Incidents such as this actually were extremely rare. Virtually all of the duty at sites such as the Command Building, the War Room, and gate-guard duty, etc., was extremely serious business – and occasionally quite dangerous. These were simply tense times for tense young men who sometimes felt the need to find ways "to let off steam."

# Chapter 13

~

# Infamous Nazis in Heidelberg

As a result of the location of the university in Heidelberg, as well as the town's revered historic location with its ancient castle on the Neckar River, Heidelberg inevitably attracted its share of the ilk of Hitler's regime in the 1930s and early '40s – even hosting the Nazi Fuhrer himself on several occasions.

### Joseph Goebbels

In 1935, Hitler's notorious Minister of Propaganda – Joseph Goebbels – attended the dedication ceremony of a special amphitheater (called *"Thingstatte"*) in the hills above Heidelberg. *Thingstatte* was the old Germanic term for *"place of assembly."* In ceremonies at these sites, the Nazis sought to link their doctrines to ancient Germanic tradition, including, inexplicably, reverence for things like the sun.

The *Thingstatte* amphitheater above Heidelberg was designed as well for Nazi mass choral plays celebrating *"Germanness."* This site still exists as of this writing and is located just beyond a summit across the Neckar River from Heidelberg known as *"Heiligenberg,"* a noted historic site itself with remnants of prehistoric structures.

Interestingly, the Heidelberg *Thingstatte* is amazingly similar to the Nazi amphitheater portrayed in the Academy Award-winning motion picture – *The Sound of Music*.

In 1945, ten years after attending

Just like the gutter rat that he was, Joseph Goebbels, Hitler's notorious Minister of Propaganda, scurried into hiding in 1945 during the final days of the Third Reich. He is pictured here, however, at the peak of his powers, glaring threateningly at the cameraman. He did not appreciate being captured on film.

the ceremony in Heidelberg, with Germany in ruins and Hitler dead from a self-inflicted gunshot wound to the head, Goebbels, in accordance with Hitler's will, succeeded him as Chancellor of Germany. He served but one day, however in this post. The following day, he and his wife committed suicide, after having poisoned their six children with cyanide.

Photographed in 1935 by a Nazi staff photographer, the "Thingstatte" was built by students at the University of Heidelberg for use in dramatic productions celebrating the greatness of Nazi Germany. It was constructed at the site of an ancient prehistoric settlement known as Heiligenberg on the mountain across the Neckar River from Heidelberg. A ceremonial rally in progress in this photo was part of the Nazi effort to link their doctrines to ancient Germanic traditions. Notorious Nazi Propaganda Minister Joseph Goebbels attended on this night. This noted site still exists in Heidelberg.

Photographed circa 1939, during a visit to Heidelberg is notorious Fuhrer of the Third Reich Adolf Hitler (foreground in trench-coat). The Nazi Bundespost building is visible background. This photo was taken not far from the Heidelberg Bahnhof (rail depot) and the historic Hauptstrasse in that city.

UPPER PHOTO - Hitler acquired a strong backing in Heidelberg in his early rise to power, garnering 41% of the vote in the city in 1933. The Hauptstrasse leading down to the old portion of Heidelberg is visible between the two buildings to the rear. The old Bundespost (post office) is visible to the rear of Hitler's Mercedes sedan. LOWER PHOTO - Photographed in 1973, the old Bundespost building was still in existence, but the structure beside it had been replaced by Horten's department store. (Lower photo by R.O. Jackson)

## Adolf Hitler

In 1938, Hitler paid a formal visit to the city. His National Socialists had garnered only 25% of the vote in the election of 1930, but 41% in the following election.

In his visit, Hitler, among other things, reviewed a contingent of troops near Bismarkplatz and the old Bundespost (post office) in downtown Heidelberg not far from the Hauptstrasse. The Bundespost building still stood as of the 1970s, as did many other buildings from Hitler's era.

The purpose of the Nazi Fuhrer's 1938 visit or whether his trip required him to overnight in the town is unknown today. In all likelihood, he was enroute to another destination.

By 1938, Hitler had achieved superstar status in Germany, and the posture and attentiveness of those in his presence in this photo bespeak his importance.

## Albert Speer

The Nazi official perhaps most associated with Heidelberg was Hitler's Minister of Armaments and Architecture, Albert Speer. He was a native of Mannheim a few miles from Heidelberg. His family had lived there for generations. He had attended school in Karlsruhe near Heidelberg and apparently became fond of the Heidelberg location, since he eventually made it his home.

As a member of Hitler's inner circle during the late 1930s and early 1940s through World War II, Speer received particular renown. In the International Military Tribunal (Nuremburg Trials) at the close of World War II, he was one of the few who demonstrated remorse for his actions in service to Hitler. For that and other reasons – despite having used Jewish slave labor intensely in all his projects – he drew a relatively short

Albert Speer was a long-time member of Adolf Hitler's "Inner Circle," serving as his Minister of Armaments. Convicted of war crimes, he was sentenced to 20 years in Spandau Prison in Berlin, ironically the very site at which he had wielded so much power only a few years previous. He was the only high-ranking Nazi to admit guilt for his actions, and in doing so, was spared a harsher sentence.

prison sentence when other Nazi criminals were being hung by the neck until dead.

Speer, nevertheless, was found guilty on counts three and four (*"War Crimes"* and *"Crimes Against Humanity"*) at Nuremberg. He was sentenced to 20 years in prison and was released in 1966.

Following his release, Speer returned to a home in Heidelberg at which he had lived during his days with Hitler. It was located in the hills above the city (and still stands to this day as far as I know). When the security team from the 529th Military Police Company drove up to the CINC's residence for duty during 1972-1973, we often saw Speer sitting in

A view of the driveway and modest home of Nazi war criminal Albert Speer, former Minister of Armaments for Adolf Hitler and Nazi Germany during World War II. Following publication of his best-selling book *"Inside the Third Reich"* in 1969, Speer became a wealthy man, but continued to live modestly. In a time when most former Nazis were hiding and in seclusion, Speer made no attempt whatsoever to hide his existence, even prominently displaying his name on the stone front gate-post of his home. In 1972-1974 security guards, traveling to and from the CINC's residence in the mountains above Heidelberg and near Speer's home, often saw him resting in the courtyard of this home. (Photo by R.O. Jackson)

a shady area near his porch. I couldn't help wondering what he was thinking as he watched us pass.

Speer later became even more famous – and wealthy – with the release of his best-selling book – *Inside the Third Reich*, published in 1970, with rights later sold for a made-for-television motion picture in 1982. Since most of the individuals that were close to Hitler died or committed suicide before sharing their experiences and/or secrets regarding their activities and crimes, this book found a substantial audience of interest.

Following the release of *Inside the Third Reich* (1970), Speer penned *Spandau: The Secret Diaries* (1976). These books sold several million copies and made Speer richer-still. A third book, *Infiltration: The SS and German Armament*, was later published in the United States, adding further to Speer's wealth. Who says "Crime doesn't pay?"

Speer died on September 1, 1981, following a stroke in Britain, and was buried in Heidelberg.

# Chapter 14

## 1970s Life in Heidelberg

For their first year, those individuals assigned to the 529th were required to live in the barracks – no exceptions. The reasons for this were two-fold. Number one, the commander of the 529th wanted to be certain all newcomers were properly introduced to life in Germany before allowing them out on the general economy. Number two, that same commander wanted to make certain that a certain amount of the man-power in the 529th was available and near-at-hand 24/7. He wasn't about to get his tail in the ringer because he couldn't account for his men during an emergency.

This really was unnecessary though, because virtually no rookie soldier in Germany was interested in venturing out to live beyond the confines of the military installation anyway. There was just too much of a learning-curve.

But after that first year, a fair number of "independent souls" were champing at the bit to obtain an apartment in downtown Heidelberg or one of the suburbs. Many GIs by that point also had obtained their own transportation, which made them that much more independent.

### Nussloch Apartment

By late 1972 or early 1973, one group had moved out to the suburb of Nussloch a few miles from Heidelberg. I don't remember everyone who lived there, but I do seem to recall that

Ed Meek, Dudley Webb, John "Thumper" Thornton, and I think Jack Williams were renting a three-bedroom apartment which had been "reconfigured" into a four-person flat. When Thumper's tour of duty was up, they asked me to join them.

The Nussloch apartment cost 1,000 Deutschmarks per month, which was the rough equivalent of approximately $363.00 per month. Poor as G.I.s were in the early 1970s, that $363.00 split five ways was approximately $75.00 per month for each of us. As little as that is today, in 1973 when I moved into the apartment, $75.00 was a significant sum of money.

I had no vehicle at the time, so I – and most everyone else – was dependent upon a multi-colored Volkswagen Beetle which Meek - and I think Thornton – had collectively purchased. That "Bug" made the rounds too – all over Germany and regularly back and forth to downtown Heidelberg. And just like most all the other Volkswagens, it rarely gave a mechanical problem. It just ran and ran and ran, all with virtually no mechanical service.

American cigarettes, understandably, were highly, highly-valued by the Germans, but virtually unavailable to them. These tobacco items, therefore, were almost like gold on the German economy. In the early 1970s, every G.I. had a certain number of "tobacco coupons" which authorized that

CITY MAP OF HEIDELBERG

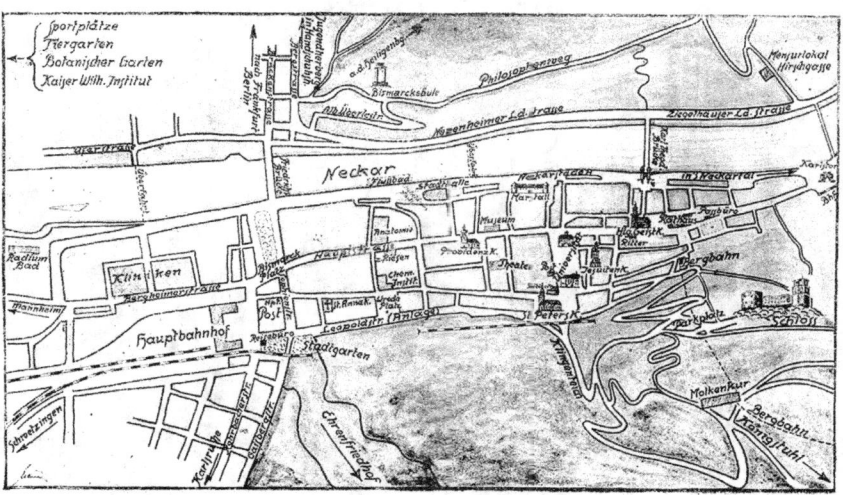

A hand-drawn map of Heidelberg. This once-small college town with its historic castle on the scenic Neckar River has grown by leaps and bounds since the 1970s.

G.I. to purchase cigarettes for very little cost. As a result, cigarettes became our black-market currency.

Since I didn't use tobacco, I saved up my tobacco coupons every month. Long story short, I was practically able to pay my portion of the rent each month solely with cigarettes. Had it not been for that, I would not have been able to live off-post, because most all of my paycheck each month was sent back home to Georgia to re-pay my civilian education loans for the tuition, fees and housing costs during my initial days at the University of Georgia.

I don't recall exactly why we departed Nussloch, but at some point, that residence was no longer a viable option for us. Perhaps the landlord

*And just like most all the other Volkswagens, it rarely gave a mechanical problem.*

– who lived up above us – eventually tired of our constant loud music blaring from our over-sized speakers and stereo systems. Or maybe we just lost enough GIs to rotations back to the states that the monthly rent was no longer feasible. Whatever the circumstances, we left.

### Hauserstrasse Apartment

I think I moved back into the 529th Barracks for a short while after departing the Nussloch apartment, but in September of 1973, according to a letter I wrote back home to my mother, I had moved to another apartment nearer to the 529th barracks. This time, it was a third-floor flat on Hauserstrasse.

This new apartment cost considerably less – and was a better

89

For many years, troops at the 529th M.P. Company patronized a beer hall known loosely as "Zill's," but formally named "Zillertal." It was such an institution for many years in the 529th that "Mama" - who ran the place - even had a manikin dressed in an old M.P. uniform in one corner inside. (Notice the guy at far left scratching his stomach.) (Photo by R.O. Jackson)

A view from the vicinity of Bismarkplatz looking down the entrance to the Hauptstrasse in the old section of Heidelberg near the famous castle. This was where all the food, fun, and females were located in the 1970s, so when not on duty, many Deuce-Niners literally lived in this neighborhood. (Photo by R.O. Jackson)

Back in the days when "disco" was king – or "queen," however one wishes to look at it, this was yet another haunt of some Deuce-Niners. It was also located in the old section of Heidelberg near the Hauptstrasse and the Neckar River. (Photo by R.O. Jackson)

unit – at only 480 marks per month, split three ways, meaning I was now paying 175 marks (approximately $58.00) per month. And this time, I definitely did pay for it all in cigarettes.

Les Toon, Jim Hewitt, and I lived in this three-bedroom, one-bath, third-floor walk-up. I don't recall who replaced Hewitt when his tour of duty expired several months later, but when Toon and the other guy departed, I recruited Gene Sauls, Kevin McCooe, and Dave Brands (reconfiguring one of the rooms into a two-man room) as co-renters, and was now paying even less rent (approximately $44.00 per month).

Now some of you might be thinking at this point, why would one move "off-post" where one not only had to

A contingent of the Nazi Wehrmacht - probably the 110th Infantry Regiment which was housed in the facilities which later became Campbell and Patton Barracks – goose-step near the Hauptstrasse in Heidelberg, Germany in 1939. Notice ancient Heidelberg castle on the mountain in the background. Deuce-Niners from the 529th spent a great deal of time in this vicinity from the 1950s to 2012, and it was sometimes difficult to accept that the same sites were also once occupied by the troops of Nazi Germany.

Heidelberg, with its very scenic locale and safety provided by the multitude of USAREUR troops, became the setting for a major motion picture in 1948. *I Was a Male War Bride* was a 1949 comedy directed by Howard Hawks. Movie icons Cary Grant and Anne Sheridan pose for the camera during a break in filming. Note the information packet the pair are reviewing is identified as "Heidelberg Military Post." The actual location at which this photo was snapped in Heidelberg is unknown today.

pay rent (as little as it was), but also purchase food for and prepare one's own meals (since the chow-hall was an inconvenient ride back to the barracks). Well, the answer is two-fold. Number one, it allowed one to generally avoid the NCOs and officers of the 529th's billets who just naturally imposed a restrictive environment for enlisted men. Number two was "women." Those GIs who had a private apartment were imminently more likely to attract female companionship than were those stuck in the barracks. And when female company *was* acquired, one also had automatic private accommodations as well.

As one matured and moved up in rank and stature in the 529th, he became more and more adept at acquiring female companionship. The apartment at Hauserstrasse remains as a happy memory for me even today, and probably always will.

Some that I recall in particular are: a cosmetician; a student at the University of Heidelberg; and a nurse who worked right across Hauserstrasse from our apartment. The nurse was Marie Stein, and she rolled one of the wheelchair-bound patients out to the hospital's (or maybe it was a nursing home's) sun-room facing Hauserstrasse each day, and every time I saw her, I waved and gave her my most winning smile.

One special day when I caught sight of Marie, I motioned for her to come

Photographed top is a view toward the Hauptstrasse, the main street of old town Heidelberg, Germany in 1945, as U.S. Army troops enter to take command of the city.

Photographed bottom is an identical view of that same site taken in 1972, twenty-seven years after the conclusion of the war. (Lower photo by R.O. Jackson)

up to the apartment – and, to my utter amazement, she did. It pains me today to imagine these young attractive and exciting females from 1973 who now are in their 70s....but I chasten these thoughts with the fact that they'd think the same thing about me.

There was a large sports park with manicured landscaping, an Olympic-size swimming pool and a diving platform, a small snack shop, and other attractions not far from where we lived. We often took our lady-friends there to enjoy the sun and swim in the pool on our off-days.

I liked to dive, and one day I wanted to try out that Olympic diving platform. It didn't look excessively high from the ground, but when one climbed up that ladder to the platform, it suddenly looked like one was standing on the moon.

Diving was the easy part; when I hit that swimming pool, however, at a speed in the neighborhood of Mach-4, it completely stripped my swim trunks off of me, necessitating a quick recovery from the bottom of the pool.

## Famous Tourists

Heidelberg, with its scenic setting on the Neckar River has been a favorite haunt of more than one celebrity over the years. Notwithstanding those in the motion picture industry such as **Cary Grant** and **Anne Sheridan** who starred in the 1949 Howard Hawks production – *I Was a Male War Bride* – which was filmed on location in Heidelberg, numerous other VIPs have enjoyed its environs.

In 1878, a by-then famous **Mark Twain** visited and resided in the old town for several months. Both hotels in which he had accommodations still stand today.

Twain particularly enjoyed taking a

German prisoners being marched for transport to a prisoner-of-war camp. This photograph was snapped in 1945 at the historic Kornmarkt (ancient Corn Market Plaza) near the historic Hauptstrasse in the old section of Heidelberg, Germany.

stroll and writing along the nature path called *"Philosopher's Way"* on the hillside above the old bridge on the opposite side of the Neckar River from the town. He reportedly wrote virtually all of *"A Tramp Abroad"* (1880) at this site.

Twain also delighted in spending time at the old castle on the hillside above Heidelberg. His character – Huckleberry Finn – is believed to have been at least partially drawn from the wild blueberries found there. The German word for "huckleberry" is "heidelbeere," and the word "Heidelberg" roughly translated from German to English means "Huckleberry Mountain" Heidel (huckle) berg (mountain).

Twain also enjoyed supping at the 16th Century Red Ox Inn in old-town Heidelberg on the Hauptstrasse. This famous eatery is still open as of this writing in 2023.

In 1950, famed writer **Ernest Hemingway** also spent time in Heidelberg, enjoying the Tyrolean beer. Inspired, he returned to Cuba and wrote *"The Garden of Eden"* and the middle section of *"Islands in the Stream."*

# Chapter 15

## The "Frauenhausen"

There were plenty of Deuce-Niners – and other military personnel – who simply were unable to attract female companionship. And though it is a somewhat "sensitive" subject, the satisfaction of the "needs" of these men was, nevertheless, a basic necessity of life, particularly the life of a soldier.

In the 1970s in Heidelberg, things were no different than they are today. Most men need women, and if soldiers in Heidelberg couldn't attract the companionship of a steady date, they used the other option. Yeah. That's right. I'm talking about the local "cat-house." The house of ill repute. The *"House of the Rising Sun."*

Interestingly, prostitution was legal in Heidelberg when I arrived in 1972. I, of course knew not then nor now anything about this industry first-hand. I received all of my information "second-hand." And yes. . . I hear you people responding "Rightttttttt."

Prostitution has in fact been legal in Germany for many years. The Germans – and indeed many Europeans – just consider it to be a practical solution to a common need. For that and other reasons, it essentially is a legal "business."

In order for this "industry" to be and remain problem-free, special health officials routinely checked and maintained control on all of these "businesses." The houses – known loosely as "frauenhausen" or "house of women,"

are all required to be identified and registered with the German government which conducts annual health inspections of all the females and requires certain health standards in order for these "frauenhausen" to remain in "business."

The "cat-house" in Heidelberg was located not far from the Heidelberg bahnhof (train station) shortly before one reached the U.S. Army PX. Every male in Heidelberg knew where it was. This location made total sense business-wise. The "ladies" not only were able to take advantage of any traffic arriving by train, but also of the endless stream of GIs making daily use of the PX.

I have been told that the Heidelberg cathouse was of an unusual architectural design too. Inside, a spiral staircase supposedly took one up approximately five or six levels – round and round – where small rooms branched off from the spiral on both sides. One apparently walked up the stairs, looked over the "merchandise," then made a selection.

I have also been told these ladies were quite beautiful, essentially because 1/ they didn't consider their profession to be morally wrong, and 2/ most of any risk had been removed by the health requirements of the practice and the annual medical exams, and 3/ – and this is the kicker – I have been told these ladies made a fortune, and in 2012, I suspect there were quite a few beautiful but sad faces too, when the U.S. Army pulled out of Heidelberg forever.

## Chapter 16

~

# A Trip to Spain

I don't know who came up with the idea. Three friends and I were sitting around our apartment off-post one day when we decided we should take a trip to some exotic location we had not yet visited in our travels. After all, we were in "Europe." We had ample time on our hands and it might be a long, long, time – if ever – that we would have this opportunity again.

One of those guys eventually came up with the idea of taking a trip to Spain. I had already been to France several times, as well as Belgium, Holland, Austria, Scotland, and a number of other places, but never to Spain, so that choice suited me just fine. Our "travel planner" got to work on the logistics.

By that point in our lives, many of us had our own transportation. One of the great things about Germany is that even a poor GI can obtain quite a nice "ride" there for considerably less than the same vehicle might cost in the United States. And if one had a "connection" – for instance a used car dealer who eagerly sought "American cigarettes" as most Germans did, since they were unable to obtain them on the open market without paying exorbitant prices, then

one could obtain a reasonably nice car at even less cost.

As had my other friends with "transportation," I had opted for a moderate vehicle – the Volkswagen – because it was so prevalent in Germany, and the prices therefore were extremely reasonable for a "used Volkswagen." I also didn't want to spend a lot of money, because I had heard from other GIs that the cost of shipping a vehicle back home was prohibitive for lowly enlisted personnel. I think I wound up spending in the neighborhood of $300.00 on that car. Now I know that almost sounds like pocket change today, but adjusting for inflation, $300 in 1972 was the rough equivalent of approximately $1,950.00 today, so it wasn't dirt-cheap.

Despite the fact that it was a "used car," the Volkswagen I ultimately purchased was virtually new except it had a door on one side which had been replaced. And when I say "new," I mean almost "brand new." I had gotten quite a deal because, as explained earlier, I was not a tobacco user, so I had saved up "black-market" cigarettes equaling approximately $125.00 in value.

When the day came to pick up my

*We had ample time on our hands and it might be a long, long, time – if ever – that we would have this opportunity again.*

new car, I was thrilled. And needless to say, when the day that my tour of duty in the Army was complete and I had to return to "the world," I almost cried when I had to leave that car behind. I wound up donating it to a good friend – who was as thrilled as was I when I had purchased it. But I digress. . . .

We set out driving across Belgium, then France, and eventually down the Mediterranean Coast to the Spanish Riviera. The destination we had chosen was Barcelona and "Casa del Sol" on the Mediterranean. We'd be able not only to enjoy the Riviera, but also the delights of one of the larger cities in Spain.

One of the "sights" we wanted to see was a bull-fight. Barcelona has a huge bull-fighting arena. I'd never previously been to such an event, so this was going to be a totally new experience for me.

After we arrived in the city and had gotten set up in our hotel room, we set out for the beach. We purchased leather "bota-bags" – a Spanish invention of a large pouch into which one could pour a bottle of wine which was then corked up – to float out on the Mediterranean and soak up the sun.

After a day of wine and water, we decided that the bull-fights were next on our list. When we arrived at the arena, I couldn't help but notice that all around the exterior there were scores of shops selling all manner of leather goods and fresh beef. It seemed a bit strange to me at the time, but I was still suffering from the effects of the bota-bag and sun-stroke.

At any rate, I wasn't the only one of

*We'd be able not only to enjoy the Riviera, but also the delights of one of the larger cities in Spain.*

us who hadn't been to a bull-fight. None of us in our group had. We knew only that there was a matador who "teased" a huge bull with his cape back and forth in the arena until the bull was worn out. We didn't know much more than that – at least I didn't.

As GIs are often want to do, we started on our bota-bags again that day, so we were essentially half-way through a bottle of wine before the first bull even entered the arena. Looking back, we were pretty-inexperienced young men – barely 20 years old each. We had no idea that a matador in Spain is the equivalent stature-wise of the heavyweight boxing champion in the United States.

I also didn't know that there is a "toreador" and there is a "matador" – two entirely different "animals" if you will. The toreador comes out first and does the hard work, tempting the huge bull, running him back and forth and stabbing him each time he passed with these short little barbed spears known as "banderillas" which caused a massive loss of blood from the animal. After the toreador has completely exhausted the bull, the matador then makes his appearance.

When the first toreador was introduced in the ring, we noticed that an unusual amount of cheering and respect was directed his way. I don't recall the exact circumstances, but I'm sure we were a little surprised that so much adulation was being heaped upon what appeared to us to be a sissy-looking slim man in sissy tights with a little cape – but what did we know??

With each pass, the toreador stabbed more and more of these banderillas into the bull until he soon was simply a bloody mess with the blood spattered across the bull ring's dirt field. Soon, the exhausted animal was able to do nothing but stand and stare dumbly at the toreador, obviously totally confused at how he could keep failing to eliminate his tormentor.

We of course were watching this in awe. When the bull could move no more, the matador strutted out and applied the coup de gras (coupe de grace to us) to the bull, driving a long sword between his shoulder blades down into his heart, causing him to collapse in death on the spot. We were aghast.

After this first bull was dispatched, we kinda just looked at each other. "Do they actually consider this a sport?" we inquired among ourselves. There was no sport to this. The bull essentially has no chance whatsoever. To our way of thinking, the bull just set himself up for failure while the prissy little toreadors and matadors strutted and preened for the audience's loud cheers as they dispatched the huge animals. We were disgusted.

We watched several more of these fights – all with the

> *The rampaging bull caught that toreador on his horns and, in his rage, flung him like a rag-doll several rows up into the seats.*

> *Well... This was obviously a tragic occurrence, but for some strange reason, we four GIs simply felt that, in an unusual sort of way, justice had been served.*

same results. Finally, however, something unusual happened. One of the bulls broke with the normal routine of charging the bright cape only to miss the toreador, and actually chose instead to charge directly at the man, much to his horror. The results were stunning. The rampaging bull caught that toreador on his horns and, in his rage, flung him like a rag-doll several rows up into the seats. After he came back down to earth and landed with a thud and a bang in the seats, that poor toreador didn't move an inch. When they carried him off on a stretcher, he was still unconscious.

Well... This was obviously a tragic occurrence, but for some strange reason, we four GIs simply felt that, in an unusual sort of way, justice had been served. Americans quite often will pull for the underdog in a fight – even if it's a bull. And if ever there was a true facsimile of an underdog in this contest, it was definitely these bulls who were so easily being dispatched and then dragged from the ring.

Now when the toreador was flung up into the stands, a total hush came over the thousands in the crowded arena. As far as they were concerned, their "hero" had been totally un-expectedly crushed. They were devastated.

We Americans, on the other hand, responded quite differently. One can only imagine the surprise and outrage of the Spaniards when, about two-thirds of the way up in the arena, four Americans are loud-ly cheering and clap-ping in acclamation for the bull. I'm sure they were thinking *"What in the hell is going on? We will keel them!"*

It was at about this time that five or six young "toughs" sitting up behind us began throwing half-filled containers at us and openly challenging us to fight. By this point, we had all run through the contents of our bota-bags, so we were pretty-well hammered, and unaware of the growing danger around us.

One of the Spaniards pulled what looked to be about a two or three-foot-long knife from his belt and held it threateningly in his hand. In reality, that knife was probably only about a 10 or 12-inch blade, but still a very, very dangerous weapon in the hands of someone who knew how to use it.

The knife-wielding Spaniard and his friends began slowly advancing on us and we began to take up drunken defensive poses. Even though we'd been taught in Basic Training how to disarm a knife-wielding opponent, that training was little more than a distant memory at that moment. We, for the most part, were in La La Land.

At about this same time – and to this day I don't remember which one of

> *This obviously seemed so absurdly ridiculous to the challengers that they all suddenly burst out laughing – great big belly-laughs.*

us it was – but stagger-ing a bit, he held up his hand to halt the Span-iards' advance by say-ing "Wait!! Wait!! Wait!!... I'm not ready!"

I don't know if our opponents had any idea what he was say-ing (probably not), but they almost certainly could understand the universal language of the raised hand signal-ing one to "Wait," so they paused, smiling to themselves. My friend then reached into his pocket, pulled out a tiny (and I do mean "tiny") little one-inch pen-knife, and, taking his time, very methodically opened it up with two daintily-extended fingers, then held it up and very drunkenly motioned the Span-iards to come get us.

This obviously seemed so absurd-ly ridiculous to the challengers that they all suddenly burst out laughing – great big belly-laughs. I'm certain they had to have been thinking "Crazy Americans." This kept up for several minutes.

As the Spaniards continued to hoot and roll, those around them began laughing as well. Luckily for us, at about this same time, a pair of attentive Span-ish Federales (police) came strolling up and we at least had the good sense to tactfully leave under their escort.

Needless to say, our impression of a Spanish bull-fight took a noticeable "hit" that day, falling to the absolute bot-tom of our list as far as righteous "sports" were concerned. We left shortly thereaf-ter to return to Germany – a little old-er, and a little wiser. We also threw away those dern bota-bags.

# Chapter 17

## Deuce-Nine Leadership

L est you, the reader herewith, be deceived that the accomplishments and successes of a unit such as the 529th Military Police Company are automatic, please allow us to bring you up to speed on the importance of the leadership therein. The line-MPs and their support groups are one thing, but they wouldn't exist without the intelligence, management, and special skills of the officers and NCOs who lead them.

The 529th's successes during the decade of the 1970s began with individuals such as the late Col. Charles Shay, post commandant at Patton Barracks for many years and the "top dog" in the Deuce-Nine. It was individuals such as Col. Shay who advised and led the likes of Captains Bogema, Case, Enger, Redding, and numerous other Deuce-Nine commanders throughout the years. Many of these men were West Point graduates, intelligent, seasoned, and skilled beyond the norm, who demonstrated their mettle time and time again both at this duty station and at others into the future.

Most civilians never consider the fact that a successful and outstanding military unit requires leaders

*Every aspect of a streamlined and successful military unit must mesh perfectly with every other aspect.*

who are equally outstanding and dedicated to their assignment(s) and their country, with the unusual management skills required to accomplish what many would consider unreachable goals. Every aspect of a streamlined and successful military unit must mesh perfectly with every other aspect. Any failure along the line can and will cause the entire effort to fail.

Talented and successful company commanders are those who have recruited talented and successful executive officers and other staff to coordinate the various aspects of an award-winning unit such as the 529th Military Police Company. I remember quite clearly how lieutenants Wise, Anderson, Kennedy, King, Markardt and others were clearly more advanced in intelligence, capability, and dedication than many others of their rank at that time, and the 529th was fortunate to have them. That circumstance, however, was not happenstance.

And lest we forget the "heart and soul" of any military unit, a successful mission accomplishment does not occur without talented and dedicated non-commissioned officers. These are the men who actually put into action and operation the orders and instructions of the officer cadre, and who make certain those instructions are carried out to a "T."

The 529th was doubly-blessed in that regard. Many of those impressive NCOs are no longer with us today, and there's a reason for that... They were all seasoned soldiers, well-trained and well-experienced in their particular skills and technical expertise. The late SSG Boehinke, 1SG Hamblin, 1SG Hendricks, SSG Parrish, and 1SG Templeton, to name just a few, come to mind when I think back to the men who put the Deuce-Nine head and shoulders above other military police units worldwide.

### Outstanding NCOs

There were in fact innumerable NCOs in the 529th during the decade of the 1970s. During the early '70s when I was there, many of these individuals were exceptional soldiers; others not so much. Some of the more qualified and highly-respected ones which I recall were SFC Kenneth Leece, SFC Henry, SSG Thomas, SGT Frank Withers, 1SG Hendricks, SSG Ted Lawrence, SGT "Penny" Harrington, SGT Ed Cormican, SSG Patrick Mackay, and SGT Bob Waller to name just a few. The experienced careers

> *They were all seasoned soldiers, well-trained and well-experienced in their particular skills and technical expertise.*

> *I've seen the Army's mountain training facility for the Rangers in north Georgia... the word "challenging" comes to mind.*

of Hendricks, Henry, Lawrence, Leece, Mackay, Thomas and others provided them with an added edge for professionalism. Others, such as Withers, Harrington, Waller, and Cormican were but a few years older than the enlisted men at that time, a situation which just naturally allowed for a good working relationship as well.

When I arrived at the 529th in 1972, Sgt. Frank Withers was already well-established within the Company. He was only a buck-sergeant at that time, but he was an Airborne Ranger with "ribbons" and two tours in Vietnam under his belt. He was also a member of the USAREUR "Color Guard." Those qualifications carried a lot of weight among raw troops and still do even today I'm sure. Airborne Ranger status ain't easy to come by. I've seen the Army's mountain training facility for the Rangers in north Georgia... the word "challenging" comes to mind.

As explained, in the early 1970s, Frank wasn't much older than most of us enlisted men. We were all in our early twenties and I think Frank was in his late twenties. As a result, he socialized to a large degree with enlisted men; he didn't circulate to any great degree among the non-commissioned officers.

The reasoning was simple. Just as with

SGTs Harrington, Waller and Cormican, Frank simply had more in common with the enlisted men than he did with 40 and 50-year-old NCOs. One could only find it ironic today, that Frank ultimately became one of those elderly highly placed NCOs himself, rising to the rank of First Sergeant, which is but one rank below Sergeant Major and two ranks below Command Sergeant Major, the highest NCO rank possible in the Army. *(There's also obviously a "Sergeant Major of the Army" if one wishes to get technical, but it's more of an appointed than earned rank.)*

As a result, anyone who happened to be working Frank's shift generally considered himself lucky. There was always a lot of camaraderie and minimal stress on Frank's shift, simply because he had an easy-going personality. It wasn't that he was irresponsible either; far from it. He just placed a high value upon friendship.

With the regular line-NCOs, it usually was a different story. Most of them were essentially inflexible about the simplest of issues and interested only in their pursuit of a higher rank. Though this was very understandable since they were career-Army, it nevertheless made the task of working with them less than appealing to virtually all the enlisted men.

*There was always a lot of camaraderie and minimal stress on Frank's shift, simply because he had an easy-going personality.*

*They were all proud of their station in life and pursued their jobs with professionalism and determination which exceeded the norm.*

I still consider Frank Withers a good friend, even today, half a century removed from our days in Heidelberg.

And when push came to shove – as on May 24, 1972 – "when the going got tough, the tough got going." None of the cadre faltered in leadership on that fateful day following an almost unspeakable horror. They immediately activated emergency procedures which quickly brought to a close and resolved a very tragic event.

There is a reason that units such as the 529th excel where others remain mediocre. The men and the might of the Deuce-Nine were the cream of the crop in the decade of the 1970s, and that tradition continues to the present-day. They, however, had an additional characteristic. They were all proud of their station in life and pursued their jobs with professionalism and determination which exceeded the norm.

Contrary to present-day attitudes toward the U.S. military which is highly admired and respected (with good reason) everywhere, the men of the 529th maintained a significant esprit de corps at a time when the Army was routinely scorned everywhere. When it came to "esprit de corps," the 529th was the workhorse of the U.S. Army.

## Chapter 18

*❧*

# The Army's Finest

On September 10, 1974, the commander of the 529th Military Police Company was notified that the "Deuce-Nine" was the winner of the prestigious *"Brigadier General Jeremiah P. Holland Award"* recognizing the top military police unit – company size or smaller – in the entire United States Army. This was a competition among upwards of some 200 military police units worldwide, with the requirements stipulated in AR 672-11, and the 529th had won it all, hands-down.

Ironically, in what should have been one of the finest hours of the 529th, very little in the way of personal recognition, unfortunately, was ever actually directed to the men of the unit for this accomplishment. An article on the Deuce-Nine's award did appear in *Stars & Stripes* and several other newspapers, and the trophy was officially presented by the Commander-in-Chief of the United States Army in Europe – General Michael S. Davison – to the commander of the Deuce-Nine – Captain James Case – but the troops themselves never witnessed the trophy or its presentation; they never received an official unit citation as a result of the award; nor anything else. Most never even knew the award existed. And it was the men of the 529th who were the heart and soul of this immense achievement.

At the very least, a unit citation should have been issued which could have been officially worn on the uniforms

Gen. Michael S. Davison, commander-in-chief of the United States Army in Europe and the Army Commander of NATO (L), presents the "Jeremiah P. Holland Award" to Capt. James Case (R), commander of the 529th Military Police Company. The 529th was the top military police company in the United States Army, worldwide. Gen. Davison commanded over 270,000 troops in Europe at this time. (Photo by Bob Walls)

of the 529th, but no such award was ever issued. To some degree, this quite probably was emblematic of the times, and the morale problem which existed in the United States military during the decade of the 1970s. Whether one is willing to admit it or not, during this time-period, virtually anything associated with the American military was reviled and ridiculed by civilian populations worldwide due to our nation's involvement in the Vietnam Conflict.

# Herald Post

Vol. 1, No. 7    Heidelberg Military Community    Friday, November 15, 1974

## 529th MP Company is best in Army

By John Davies

The 529th MP company, the USAREUR Honor Guard, was awarded the BG Jeremiah P. Holland Award as the best MP Company in the Army in a ceremony at USAREUR Headquarters last Friday.

GEN Michael S. Davison, USAREUR Commander in Chief, presented the award to CPT James W. Case, 529th Commander.

In remarks during the ceremony, Davison cited the MP's "professionalism and competence" and said, "You have brought great honor to the U.S. Army Europe."

BG Jeremiah P. Holland served as USAREUR Provost Marshal from 1953-1955. He retired in 1957 and subsequently donated the award to be presented each year to that MP unit, company size or smaller, that is determined by the Department of

the Army to be the best the Army has to offer.

"The award is based on everything — duty performance, mission accomplishment, community relations, law and order and discipline," said 1SG Donald W. Hendricks. "It's a big honor really. You don't get the opportunity too many times to serve with a unit that receives the award. I've got 21 years in and this is the first time," he concluded.

Last year, the Deuce-niners came in first in USAREUR competition but second in All-Army judging.

"Everyone in the company is very happy that our efforts this year have been recognized," said CPT Case. "We were especially honored to have the CINC present the award with the Chief of Staff, MG William Kraft, attending the ceremony."

The 529th is responsible for a number of duties. Besides normal

MP duties, providing gate security for Patton and Campbell Barracks in Heidelberg and for Tompkins and Kilbourne kasernes in Schwetzingen, the 529th also supplies 15 men for classified missions in Berlin and Frankfurt, provides security for sensitive areas at HQ USAREUR and handles the physical security of the CINC's quarters, aircraft and ground transportation.

A Color Guard of Deuce-niners has, during the past fiscal year, hoisted the American flag in Holland, France and Germany a total of 45 times.

The Deuce-nine 105mm Howitzer Salute Battery was responsible for the "flawless firing" of 180 rounds during FY 74, according to the citation. Salutes were fired on Memorial Day and on the death of GEN Creighton W. Abrams, former Army Chief of

*(Continued on Page 4)*

Photo by John Davis

**THE BG JEREMIAH P. HOLLAND AWARD**

★ ★ ★ ★ ★ ★ ★ ★ ★ ★ ★ ★ ★ ★ ★ ★ ★ ★ ★

A news article announcing the Jeremiah P. Holland Award presentation to the 529th Military Police Company.

But therein lies the real heart and soul of the Deuce-Nine's worthiness in being designated "the Army's finest." It wasn't the achievement of some shiny award trophy. During these years (decade of the 1970s) of rejection and scorn of the American military, the 529th was a vision of hope. It was the "pot of gold at the end of the rainbow."

When America most needed a morale booster, the Deuce-Nine never faltered. Indeed, when the men of the 529th stepped out with all of this unit's glitter, pomp and precision, one could not help but feel proud once again to be an American. There was no escaping it. It seemed to say "Hey! Wait a minute! We're not down! We just had a little hiccup. We're still here!"

And this in no way is meant as a slight against the veterans

who served in the Vietnam Conflict either - many of whom were Deuce-Niners - because they demonstrated their grit, greatness and resolve as well under extremely harsh and ill-advised circumstances. They bravely sweated, fought, bled, and died during a dark period in our nation's history. No... This simply means the 529th was a beacon of light in this time of darkness for the military in general – perhaps the brightest beacon of light available in the 1970s.

To his credit, Capt. James Case did issue a *Letter of Commendation* to the men of the Deuce-Nine to acknowledge this amazing accomplishment. It was very appropriate, since it underscored the fact that the 1974 award was not an aberration. It was in fact an affirmation of this unit's greatness.

In 1973, the

> *But therein lies the real heart and soul of the Deuce-Nine's worthiness in being designated "the Army's finest."*

Deuce-Nine had already been named "First Runner-Up" for the *Holland Award*. In 2009, it was the recipient of the *Griffin Award* acknowledging the top military police unit in Europe. And in 2012, the final year the 529th was headquartered in Heidelberg, it was again named "First Runner-Up" for the *Holland Award* in the worldwide competition.

The *Holland Award* is anything but a "hollow award" too. This competition is open not only to all active-duty United States Army military police units company size or smaller – including those performing combat support, physical security, correctional (prison) supervision, maintenance of law and order, criminal investigation, or other military police duties – but also to the Army National Guard MP units as well as Army Reserve MP units. It is no small achievement to emerge the victor in this award.

The requirements for winning the *Holland Award*, as stated in AR 672-11, are based upon weapons proficiency (personnel qualifying as: weapons "Expert," weapons "Sharpshooter," weapons "Marksman," as well as those failing to qualify at all); physical fitness; skills preparedness: leadership qualities; non-commissioned officer education; general military education; civilian education achieved;

*It was very appropriate, since it underscored the fact that the 1974 award was not an aberration.*

*This was what actually set the Deuce-Niners during the decade of the 1970s head and shoulders above all the competition.*

reenlistments; other unit awards achieved; individual awards; unit discipline; foundations of excellence; external evaluations; and much more.

But as stated above, neither the *Holland Award* nor the *Griffin Award*, nor any other "award" represented the real reason the Deuce-Nine was justified for being ranked as "the top military police company in the Army worldwide" during the 1970s. No sir. It was this unit's commitment to military excellence, its public display of precise highly-trained troops, and its unceasing demonstration of pride in the Army and our nation's world image when those commodities were in extremely short supply in America. This was what actually set the Deuce-Niners during the decade of the 1970s head and shoulders above all the competition.

And that would be the message of this publication. Within the pages which you have just perused, we've had fun with the 529th and its men, but the Deuce-Nine – like no other Army unit – consistently made one proud to be a member of the American military at a time when that not only was extremely unpopular, but extremely difficult. It is that standard of excellence and imagery which consistently places the members of this unit – both past and present – at the top of the list in the American military.

# Chapter 19

## Odds and Ends

**Chow Hall Memories** - Okay. Let's take a vote... How many of you remember the chow hall? Hands up. Okay, how many of you remember those unbelievable ham, cheese, onions, peppers, steak, tomatoes, mushroom, and on and on omelets? That's what I thought. Pretty memorable. MPs usually just naturally appreciate the chow hall anyway, because they're coming in off duty at all hours of the day and night, hungry, tired, and ill-tempered, and the delicious smells that hit you as soon as you entered the chow hall just picked you up and instantly made you feel better. The chow hall just up the street from the Deuce-Nine was that memorable.

**Stolen Possessions** - How many of you finished your tour of duty and returned home to await the shipment of all that great stuff – quadrophonic stereo amplifiers, top-of-the-line reel-to-reel tape players, hundreds of classic stereo albums you had collected, some great collector's items you had scarfed up on the countryside, and on and on? How many of you finally received shipment of that big wooden crate bound with metal ties and couldn't wait to get it open? And how many of you got it open, only to discover that most of your possessions had been pilfered and stolen somewhere in mid-shipment? How many of you were apoplectic when you realized what had happened? Yep. Me too.

**Pop's** – How many of you wound up slipping across Kircheimer Weg to Pop's to get one of those great sub sandwiches and a bottle of cheap wine at 12:00 am on Friday and Saturday nights? Yep. Thought so. Though I always wondered about the "quality-control" involving those sandwiches, when one was hungry as all get-out late at night when no other "food" was available, they (the sandwiches) were unbelievably tasty.

**Fried Egg Sandwiches** – How many of you remember how good those warm fried egg sandwiches, seasoned with mayonnaise, tasted when the NCOIC brought them out to the CINC's quarters for a mid-night meal??? After spending six of the twelve hours of a duty-shift at the CINC's, I always had an incredible hunger, and those sandwiches really hit the spot.

**Souvenirs Taken Home** – How many of you took Nazi Germany souvenirs back home with you when you departed? I clearly recall acquiring a Nazi helmet which had been discovered – among scores of others – either in an attic of one of the buildings at Campbell or one of the bars downtown. I don't recall exactly where they came from, but they were discovered in 1973. Mine, unfortunately, never made it home with me, falling victim to the thieves who ransacked my possessions after they supposedly were securely sealed – with steel bands

– in the great wooden crates in which all our possessions were shipped back home to the states.

**Extreme "Barn Find" – How many of** you remember SPEC-4 Randy Duval? In 1973, Randy made the automobile "barn-find of a lifetime" in Heidelberg regarding Volkswagens, but I don't think he ever knew it. I'm referring to a "Beetle" for which he had obtained ownership which was an unbelievable "windfall." I don't know where Randy found this "Bug," but I seem to recall that either a German mother or wife had it stored away in a garage from either a son or a husband that she had lost. The car had barely been used, and was a high-end 1969 (or somewhere thereabouts) "sports model" Volks. It had all the "bells and whistles" too. It was a convertible; had the nice 1600 cc engine and except for perhaps a few hundred miles of use, was brand-new. And Randy obtained it for little more than a "song." I have always wondered what happened to that vehicle.

# Chapter 20

# 1970s Deuce-Nine Officers

Listed below are names of officer-rank individuals who served with the 529th Military Police Company in Heidelberg, Germany, during the decade of the 1970s. Though we have made every effort to locate and list all officers from this period who served with the 529th, there simply were not records nor memories sufficient to include all the cadre. If your name isn't listed below, we humbly apologize, but we made a determined effort to include everyone. If any information about you is incorrect, we humbly apologize for that as well. We have used the only and most recent information available. If you would please send any corrections and/or additional names or information to whippoorwillpubs@gmail.com, we will do our best to include it in any revised edition of this work.

Anderson, 1st LT Carey, 1352 Ironstone Dr., Boyer, PA, 19512 (canderson@dekabatteries.com)

Bledsoe, 2nd LT Buddy

Bogema, Capt. Gary W., 15210 CR 602, RR 1, Danbury, TX, 77534 (gbogey18@hotmail.com)

Case, Capt. James W.

Enger, Capt. David, 640 Hillside Dr., E., Seattle, WA, 98112

Fletcher, 1st LT William J.

Kennedy, 1st LT James S.

King, 1st LT Cecil J., 3132 Kirby Smith, Wilmington, NC, 28403

Markardt, 1st LT Steve, P.O. Box 4646, Alexandria, VA, 22303 (XGFolk@comcast.net)

McCloskey, 2nd LT Leo

Redding, Capt. James Keith (deceased)

Shay, Col. Charles (deceased)

Sondervan, 2nd LT William W.

Sullivan, 1st LT Denis R.

Wellman, 1st LT Gerald L.

Wise, 1st LT Richard W., 397 Creary Street, Pensacola, FL, 32507 (rwhittenw@gmail.com)

# Chapter 21

# 1970s Deuce-Nine NCOs

Listed below are names of non-commissioned (NCO) officers who served with the 529th Military Police Company in Heidelberg, Germany, during the decade of the 1970s. We have done everything in our power to list every NCO who served during this period of time, but records for these individuals have been very limited and sketchy. Many, we fear, are also deceased. If your name isn't listed below, we humbly apologize. We did the best we could. If any information regarding you or your address is incorrect, we will include corrected information in any revised edition of this publication. Corrected information should be forwarded to: whippoorwillpubs@gmail.com.

Adams, SGT Lemuel

Adams, SFC William A.

Aiello, SGT Michael L.

Ambriz, SGT Robert

Berry, SFC John Henry  (deceased)

Bloodworth, SGT Dale G.

Boehinke, SSG Hans  (deceased)

Braggs, SPEC-6 King E.

Brown, SGT Edward J.

Burnside, SFC William A., 6901 Circle Cr. Dr., Pinellas Park, FL, 33781 (Esftumbler@tampabay.it.com)

Camillo, SSG Vasco

Chansler, SGT Stephen L.

Clark, SGT Richard L.

Coleman, MSG John, 5170 Greenbriar Dr., West Bloomfield, MI, 48323 (colemanjb1@sbcglobal.net)

Collins, SGT Billy R.

Cormican, SGT Edward P. "Fast Eddie" (deceased)

Davis, SGT James L.

Dice, SFC John H.

Duenas, SSG Alfred G.

Duffield, SGT Theodore R., 8132 State Hwy 317, Belton, TX 76513

Fisher, SGT Ronnie D.

Grey, Jr., SGT Donald

Hamblin, 1SG Ralph  (deceased)

Harrington, SGT "Penny"

Hartzell, SGT James C.

Herringa, SGT Phillip H.

Hendricks, 1SG Don W.

Hicks, SFC

Hill, SSG Terry, P.O. Box 339, Jal, New Mexico, 88252 (terry@usermail.com)

Horne, SSG Michael A.

Hussey, SGT Harry W.

Jaramillo, SPEC-5 Tony

Johnson  SGT Sam T., 1340 Kent Ave., Montrose, CO

Jones, SGT Rickey H.

Knapp, SFC Guido

Leece, SFC Kenneth Robert

Little, SGT Ronald L.

Mackay, SSG Patrick B., 9210 Village Green Blvd, Pewee Valley, KY, 40056

Marcey, SSG George Roshia (deceased)

Martinez, SGT Manuel

McLarney, SFC Clifford L.

Morgan, SSG Joe

Morris, SGT Grady D.

Nagel, SGT Alvin V.

Oldham, SGT Eric, Nashville, TN

Palmertree, SGT Gwendol L.

Parrish, SSG Willie Odell (deceased)

Patton, SGT Paul V.

Quintanilla, SGT Jesse

Ravago, SFC Aranda

Roberts, SGT Randy, 2100 Rock Rose Court, Westlake, TX 76262-4821 (roberts9@hotmail.com)

Sands, SFC John H. (deceased)

Shelley, SFC Morris J. (deceased)

Sibley, SSG Arthur L.

Slicker, SSG Paul Edward (deceased)

Spikes, SSG Lonnie, 8610 S. Maryland Pkwy, Las Vegas, NV, 89123

Stern, Spec-5 Charles E.

Story, SSG

Strickler, SSG Gary W.

Tatro, SGT Theodore W.

Taylor, SGT Sammie L.

Templeton, 1SG Sanford

Thomas, SSG

Thurman, SFC Thomas Paul (deceased)

Tipton, Sr., SGT William Kenneth (deceased)

Tyler, SFC Willis L.

VanDeventer, SGT Lloyd Mike (deceased)

Vanwert, SGT Lawrence

Waller, SGT Bob

Ward, SGT Willie J.

Wilcox, SGT Donald L.

Withers, Sgt. Francis Carter Scruggs "Frank," 111 Deer Run, Nellysford, Virginia 22958 (fwithers2@gmail.com)

The late George Marcy stares up at the camera as he comes off duty in front of Building 103 housing the barracks of the 529th M.P. Company. (Photo by Bob Walls)

# Chapter 22

# 1970s GIs & Enlisted Deuce-Niners

Listed below is a partial record of enlisted men and GIs who served in the 529th Military Police Company in Heidelberg, Germany, during the decade of the 1970s for whom records could be located. Though we did our absolute best to include everyone, there simply were not records nor memories enough to avoid omissions. If your name isn't listed below or if any information listed with your name is incorrect, we humbly apologize, and if you'll get us that information, we will make certain it is included in an updated version of this book. Please send all new names and corrections to: whippoorwillpubs@gmail.com.

Aalberg, SPEC-4 Alexander R.

Adams, PVT2 Ellen K.

Addis, SPEC-4 Lenny, Smithfield, NC, 27577 (lja627@aol.com)

Alicea-Diaz, SPEC-4 Ana L.

Allan, PVT2 Frederick J. Jr.

Alston, SPEC-4 Shirleen

Altendorf, PVT2 Stanley J.

Anderson, SPEC-4 John F.

Anderson, PFC Mark

Anderson, SPEC-4 Steve A.

Arnett, SPEC-4 Joseph T.

Annesley, PVT2 Kerry E.

Bach, SPEC-4 John W.

Baertlein, PVT2 Robert E.

Baldwin, SPEC-4 Scott

Banks, John

Barilone, SPEC-4 Richard F.

Bastin, PVT2 Kenrick Thomas

Bauer, Terry

Beardwood, SPEC-4 Jim

Bergman, SPEC-4 Frank E.

Bing, SPEC-4 Robert J.

Bounds, SPEC-4 Michael, 661 Reddoch Dr., Jackson, MS, 39211 (michaelobounds@gmail.com)

Braggs, SPEC-6 King E.

Brandon, PVT2 Wade R.

Brands, SPEC-4 David, 1210 W. Lewis St., San Diego, CA, 92103 (dbrands72@gmail.com)

Brandsema, PVT2 Paul W.

Brass, PFC Susan K.

Breedlove, SPEC-4 Michael

Breedlove, SPEC-4 Susan

Bright, Michael J., 17142 Harbor Bluffs Cir, Apt D, Huntington Beach, CA, 92649 (brightm@aol.com)

Brinkley, Gary, 920 Glendale Park Dr., Hampton, IA, 50441

Brocksmith, SPEC-4 Terry M., 5400 Braddock Dr., Zephyrhills, FL, 33541

Brousard, SPEC-4 Derek J.

Brown, Gary

Brown, PVT2 John C.

Bruno, SPEC-4 Timothy A.

Bryant, PVT2 Barbara L.

Burns, PFC Gail A.

Carlisle, SPEC-4 Kenneth R.

Carnegie, SPEC-4 Dale F.

Carnegie, PFC Kevin J.

Carson, PVT2 Melanie S.

Casey, PVT2 Christine A.

Cavanagh, PVT2 Katherine A.

Cavinee, SPEC-4 John N.

Chason, Ron, 11000 West 131st St., Overland Park, KS, 66213 (rchason100@yahoo.com)

Clarkson, PFC Roy R.

Clime, SPEC-4 James L. "Jim," 1912 36th St., Des Moines, IA, 50310

Clutteur, SPEC-4 Charles I

Cobbs, SPEC-4 William J.

Cocco, PVT2 Daniel C.

Cook, PVT2 David A.

Cook, SPEC-4 John P.

Cooper, Jr., SPEC-4 Emmitt

Copan, SPEC-4 John

Cox, Randall, 1007 Stafford Dr., Pleasant Hill, MO, 64080

Craigen, James B., 140 Apple Tree Hill, Fitchburg, MA, 01420 (jcraigen325i@gmail.com)

Cramer, SPEC-4 Joseph L.

Crawford, Frank, P.O. Box 1013, Washougal, WA, 98671

Crenshaw, Bill

Dancer, Stan

Daniel, PVT2 Guy

Dannelley, PVT2 Don J.

Darling, PFC James C.

Davis, Linwood W., 1505 Patrick Henry Hwy, Charlotte Ct House, VA, 23923 (dlinwood50@yahoo.com)

Debarr, PVT2 Terry L.

Dehaut, SPEC-4 Francis

Dewitt, SPEC-4 Donald M.

Dolansky, PFC Gerard R.

Duck, SPEC-4 Thomas

Dunn, PVT2 David M.

Dunphy, PVT2 Robert J.

Duran, SPEC-4 Clifford R.

Durga, Spec-5 Billy C.

Durst, PFC Mark J.

Duvall, SPEC-4 Randall M. "Randy," 1285 County Road 141, Tulelake, CA 96134 (duvallfarms@cot.net)

Dyslin, PVT2 Larry D.

Eden, Bill, 134 Rachel Road, Kennewick, WA, 99338

Edgell, PFC Kethy N.

Eremea, PVT2 Keith G.

Etchason, SPEC-4 Clyde, 2950 Paradise Road, Mattoon, IL, 61938 (snappyten@yahoo.com)

Fay, John F.

Ferlauto, SPEC-4 James A.

Firnhaber, SPEC-4 Michael A.

Fitzgerald, PVT2 Kevan L.

Flach, SPEC-4 Wallace E., W7472 U.S. 12, Fort Atkinson, WI, 53538 (wallaceflach@icloud.com)

Flateau, SPEC-4 Kenneth W.

Flynn, PFC Tom

Folk, Thomas Edward, 1881 Leonard Lane, Las Vegas, NV, 89108 (noblefolk@juno.com)

Ford, PVT2 Mary H.

Forrey, SPEC-4 John W.

Franklin, SPEC-4 Alan B.

Fratamico, PFC Domenico P.

Frisby, PVT2 Andrea G.

Frizzell, SPEC-4 Robert "Bob" (rpfohio@gmail.com)

Frost, Rick, 5304 O'Connor Pass, Swartz Creek, MI, 48473 (richief151@gmail.com)

Gardner, SPEC-4 Tyrone

Geist, PVT2 Rocky L.

Gifford, SPEC-4 Bruce W.

Gillette, SPEC-4 Ronald L.

Gore, PFC Russell D.

Grady, SPEC-4 Rick, Commerce City, CO

Graham, Lowell D., 3222 Frisco Hill Rd, Imperial, MO, 63052

Graham, Robert W., 24935 Marcellus Hwy, Dowagiac, MI, 49047 (robertgraham@aep.com)

Grainger, SPEC-4 William A.

Grange, PVT2 Todd C.

Grave, SPEC-4 Kenneth V., 8202 Encinitas Cove Dr., Tomball, TX, 77375 (kbgrave@sbcglobal.net)

Green, Jr. PFC Moses

Grogan, SPEC-4 John T., 112 E. Marland Ct, Nokomis, FL, 34275 (jtgroganjr@gmail.com)

Guzman, PFC Michael

Hamblin, SPEC-4 Ralph W., 594 Preserve Lane, Grand Junction, CO, 81503 (rhamjrid@gmail.com)

Hansen, Donald M., 400 Julienton Dr., Townsend, GA, 31331

Harper, PVT2 Howard J.

Harris, SPEC-4 Kyle W., 1391 Silkwood Dr., Okemos, MI, 48064 (kylewharris@aol.com)

Hazelwood, PVT2 Donald A.

Healey, SPEC-4 James E. "Jim", 109 S. Adams Ave, McGehee, AR, 71654

Heathcock, Troy L.

Herford, PFC Richard "Rick" (deceased)

Hewitt, SPEC-4 James "Jim", Richmond, VA (deceased)

Hiles, PFC Richard G.

Hodson, SPEC-4 Marian Wayne

Holbrook, SPEC-4 Terry Alan, 401 N. Division Ave, Polo, IL, 61064 (terry.holbrook@us.army.mil)

Holt, SPEC-4 Fenton B.

Houin, SPEC-4 Kenneth, 17671 West 13th, Plymouth, IN, 46563 (ken_houin@hotmail.com)

Huff, PFC Larry

Humphrey, SPEC-4 James P.

Ives, SPEC-4 David J.

Jackson, SPEC-4 R.O., 760 Heathland Dr., Roswell, GA, 30075 (ROJthird@gmail.com)

Jakes, Daniel, 3 Lilac Ave, Apt 101, Fox Lake, IL, 60020

James, SPEC-4 David C.

Jefferson, PVT2 Danny C.

Johnson SPEC-4 Charles A.

Johnson SPEC-4 Robert C., 1120 Forest Ave, Burton, MI, 48509 (firemanbobbfd2@aol.com)

Johnson Sam

Joyner, SPEC-4 John M.

Karkos, PFC Jean M.

Kaufmar, Gustav G., 2240 W. Good Hope Rd. #30, Milwaukee, WI, 53209

Kline, SPEC-4 Robert W.

Knight, SPEC-4 Walter

Kohlmeyer, Samuel R. (kohlsam2@hotmail.com)

Kuhnly, PFC Craig A.

Lakey, SPEC-4 Bob (jrwlakey@me.com)

Lamar, PFC Brian R.

Lawson, Rodney, 2636 250th St., Marshalltown, IA, 50158

Leskie, Gerald Joseph, 3489 Clintonville Rd, Waterford, MI, 48329

Logo, PFC Richard

Long, SPEC-4 Richard M.

Love, III, PFC Clyde E., 108 Wilkinson St., Shreveport, LA, 71104

Ludwig, Jr., William R. "Bill", 5251 Leonard Pass Rd, Grants Pass, OR, 97527

Lutz, SPEC-4 James S.

Lynch, Robert A.

Macht, SPEC-4 George D.

MacIsaac, SPEC-4 Wayne, 22 Mesier Ave, S, Wappingers Falls, NY, 12590 (waynem153@aol.com)

MacMillan, John M., 6171 Coyote Canyon Rd, Apt B, Fruitland, WA, 99129

Majeske, Hank

Martin, PVT2 Henry C.

Martin, William "Bill" (billmartin927@gmail.com) and (billm@floridarealtors.org)

Martinez, PFC Richard R.

Mays, PFC Linda G.

McCooe, SPEC-4 Kevin

McLeod, Nancy Livingston, P.O. Box 4280, West Richland, WA, 99353 (nancymcleod54@aol.com)

McNeill, Clarence L., 3010 Walnut Creek Pkwy, Apt L, Raleigh, NC, 27606 (cjmcneill@aol.com)

McRae, Doug, 8659 South 3920 West, West Jordan, UT, 84088 (doubal@q.com)

Meek, SPEC-4 Ed, 4238 Porter Road, North Olmsted, OH, 44070 (porterpegs@yahoo.com)

Melendez, PVT2 Steven J.

Mercer, SPEC-4 Noah D.

Miller, PFC Byron K.

Mills, PVT2 Alphonso E.

Mirrione, PFC Robert S.

Misel, Darrell, 12534 Hideaway Park Dr., Cypress, TX, 77429 (lildogsrus@aol.com)

Moeller, PFC Robert "Bob the Duke", 602 Mission Arch Dr., Roswell, NM, 88201

Moffett, PVT2 Steve J.

Mogyorossy, PVT2 Julius E.

Monroe, Steve, 4717 Parkview Dr., #K, Lake Oswego, OR, 97035 (thumpertap@yahoo.com)

Moore, PVT2 Michael R.

Morelock, PFC Ray T.

Morgan, PVT2 Samuel W. III

Mosca, SPEC-4 Anthony "Tony"

Murdoch, Bob

Munoz-Juvera, Frank, 29863 Old Sycamore Lane, Murrieta, CA, 92563 (judy.munoz@idq.com)

Munson, SPEC-4 Thomas P.

Nelson, Thomas P., 12660 Mariner Drive, Anchorage, Alaska, 99515-3613 (tsnelson@gci.net)

Nevarez, SPEC-4 Jose A.

Newkirk, SPEC-4 George W.

Newton, SPEC-4 Alan D.

Neyhouse, SPEC-4 George E.

Nichols, SPEC-4 Daniel A. "Dan", 314 N. Third St., Girard, IL, 62640 (dnicholsbsa@yahoo.com)

Nimocks, SPEC-4 Steven A.

Noblet, SPEC-4 Michael A.

Norman, SPEC-4 Danny R., 18770 Philbrook St., Rowland Heights, CA, 91748-4846

Northcraft, PVT2 Randy W.

Obrien, PVT2 Michael P.

Pamula, SPEC-4 Leonard

Parrow, SPEC-4 Michael E.

Paul, SPEC-4 Robert W.

Payne, PFC Donald J.

Picklesimer, Alan, P.O. Box 656, Montevallo, AL, 35115 (alanpicklesimer@att.net)

Pierce, James D., 15 Redfield Pkwy, Batavia, NY, 14020 (jpierce19@rochester.rr.com)

Pittman, William, 62880 LaSalle Road, #46, Montrose, CO, 81401

Pomerenke, PFC Steven R.

Pruett, Bruce, 21055 Payton Lane, Pine Grove, CA, 95665 (brpruett@aol.com)

Pruett, Jim R., 1140 Panorama Dr. NE, Apt 405, Albany, OR, 97322

Purdue, William C.

Pyle, Spec-4 Dennis J., Broderick, CA

Quintana, Bob 7601 Benson Dr., El Paso, TX, 79915 (ngqdot@att.net)

RearicK, SPEC-4 Howard M.

Reick, PFC James M.

Reid, Michael, 2024 Rock Island St., Tucumcari, NM, 88401 (reid_susan@hotmail.com)

Rhett, SPEC-4 Jerry C.

Richardson, SPEC-4 John (deceased)

Rigsby, Henry, 2603 LaGrand St. SW, Huntsville, AL, 35801

Riney, Spec-4 Dana B., 2002 Grace St., Hannibal, MO, 63401 (driney4905@sbcglobal.net)

Roberts, Bruce H., 4180 Wanda St., Ammon, Idaho, 83406-6828

Robinson, PFC David L.

Robinson, Steve, 300 Cutlass Dr., Novato, CA, 94947

Rogasch, Helmut A., 31459 Cherry Dr., Castaic, CA, 91384

Romo, PFC Anthony J.

Runde, PVT2 Debra J.

Ross, SPEC-4 Roger W.

Russell, Sheridan T.

Sauls, PFC Eugene "Gene" Braxton, 15202 SW 155th Ter, Miami, FL, 33187

Schave, PFC Mary D.

Scott, PFC Don E.

Scott, SPEC-4 Randy L.

Scragg, SPEC-4 James E. "Jim", 5560 Barna Ave, Titusville, FL, 32780 (jscragg@cfl.rr.com)

Scroggins, SPEC-4 Joel C.

Seeman, Mike, 3225 61st Street, Shellsburg, IA, 52332

Semeral, SPEC-4 Tom, Orange Co., CA and AZ (deceased)

Shanklin, SPEC-4 Deborah A.

Shanklin, SPEC-4 Kenneth W.

Shaw, SPEC-4 Randy A.

Shepherd, Waymond

Shipman, PVT2 Timothy L.

Simmons, SPEC-4 David J., 5472 S. Ireland Way, Centennial, CO, 80015

Simon, SPEC-4 Daniel B.

Small, Ron, Commerce City, CO

Smiling, Jr. SPEC-4 Gedine B.

Smith, PFC Steven H.

Smith, PFC William E.

Spaulding, SPEC-4 Michael L.

Spry, Wilford, 15673 Spry Lane, Hillsboro, WI, 54634

Stancil, SPEC-4 Dennis R.

Stern, Spec-5 Charles E.

Stevens, SPEC-4 William M.

Stewart, PFC Diane R.

Stinnett, SPEC-4 Walter S.

Stokes, PFC James R.

Strasburg, SPEC-4 William L.

Street, SPEC-4 Steven J.

Sullivan  SPEC-4 Tom "Sully"

Sweeney, William "Bill"

Sweet, SPEC-4 Duane H.

Sweet, SPEC-4 Robert E.

Swindle  SPEC-4 Robert M.

Taylor, SPEC-4 James D.

Thornton, SPEC-4 John "Thumper", 12307 Darlington Ave., W, Los Angeles, CA, 90049

Thurman, Tom and Michele

Tipton, SPEC-4 Anthony F.

Titra, SPEC-4 Anthony R.

Toon, SPEC-4 James Leslie "Les", 461 Richards Lane, Powells Crossroads, TN, 37397 (jamesltoon@gmail.com)

Truax, PFC Edward C.

Tucker, PVT2 Samuel R.

Vaverka, PFC Robert W.

Walker, SPEC-4 Michael B.

Wallace, Kurt A., 1471 Maple Valley Rd., Greene, RI, 02827 (kwallace27@cox.net)

Walls, SPEC-4 Robert "Wally", 5291 Deland Road, Flushing, MI, 48433 (bobnbonwalls@aol.com)

Walser, Ernie, 208 Ravenwood St., Hammond, LA, 70401

Walton, Robert R., 62 W. Plumosa Lane, Apt #102, Lake Worth, FL, 33467 (bubbaw789@aol.com)

Warnock, SPEC-4 David W.

Watson, SPEC-4 Mark D., 23574 38th Ave, Mattawan, MI, 49071

Weaver, Jerry, P.O. Box 245, Salina, OK, 74365

Webb, Jr., SPEC-4 Dudley, 107 Cambridge Place, England, ARK, 72046 (peggy.webb@fda.hhs.gov)

Webb, PFC Mark A.

Weigand, SPEC-4 Albert P.

Weston, SPEC-4 Tommy J.

Wheeler, Clarence C., 1004 Massalima Dr., Panama City, FL, 32401 (ccwvnvmc@att.net)

White, SPEC-4 Aulton H.

Wiersema, SPEC-4 Donald "Dutch", 6651 SE Woodmill Pond, Ln. #4-19, Stuart, FL, 34997 or 604 Hillandale Dr., Morrison, IL, 61270

Williams, SPEC-4 Donald R.

Williams, SPEC-4 Jack R., 6504 N. 153rd St., Omaha, NEB, 68116 (jwilli1275@aol.com)

Williamson, SPEC-4 David C.

Willis, SPEC-4 Barry, Commerce City, CO

Woolery, SPEC-4 Scott T., 6931 Benwood Sq, Amarillo, TX, 79109 (wooleryscott@yahoo.com)

Wroblewski, PVT2 Stephen R.

# About The Author

R. Olin Jackson was raised in northwest Georgia, where he attended the parochial schools. In 1971, he volunteered for service in the United States Army where he was trained as a military policeman and ultimately assigned to the security detail for the U.S. Army Commander of NATO, Gen. Michael S. Davison, in Heidelberg, Germany.

Serving from 1972 to 1975, "R.O." was also a member of the USAREUR Color Guard detail from 1973-1975. In 1974, competing against upwards of 200 other U.S. Army military police units, the 529th was the recipient of the prestigious *"Brigadier General Jeremiah P. Holland Award"* as the top military police company in the United States Army worldwide.

Upon completion of his military service, R.O. was awarded the *Good Conduct Medal* and the *Army Commendation Medal* and was honorably discharged.

R.O. returned stateside where he earned a bachelor's degree in journalism from Georgia State University in 1977, and a master's degree in political science history from the University of North Georgia in 1982.

Professionally, R.O. initially landed employment as a speechwriter for a Georgia politician in 1978, moving on in the early 1980s to the University of North Georgia where he served as Director of Media Services and Sports Information.

In 1984, R.O. was employed as a senior account executive with a major public relations firm in Atlanta. In this capacity he traveled throughout the United States for clients ranging from hotel chains to national resort developers.

In 1985, R.O. founded **Legacy Communications, Inc.**, where he became the executive editor and publisher of his flagship award-winning creations – **North Georgia Journal** and **Georgia Backroads** magazines – the premier travel and history publications of Georgia. He parlayed this endeavor into a 20-year publishing career.

In the interim, R.O. also wrote/co-wrote and edited a selection of books, including *Moonshine, Murder and Mayhem in Georgia* (2003); *Tales of the Rails in Georgia* (2004); *Georgia Backroads*

*Traveler* (2005); and *Georgia's Doc Holliday* (2005).

In 2005, R.O. sold Legacy Communications and the magazines and semi-retired to manage an investment portfolio of commercial real estate. In 2021, he returned to the world of journalism, founding **Whippoorwill Publications, LLC.**

R.O.'s creations at Whippoorwill have included *Mystery & History in Georgia, Volume I* (2022) which was recently honored with a *Five-Star Award* by **Readers' Favorite** book awards, and the companion to that book: *Mystery & History in Georgia, Volume II* (2023). These and other works by R.O. are available on Amazon.com, IngramSpark.com and other fine booksellers.

Other creative works include *Some Genealogy Keys to Some Georgia Family Trees* (2023) which provides detailed historic and genealogical information on ten interrelated Georgia families: the Neels, Andersons, Fricks, Hudgins, Tanners, Jordans, Gravatts, Pettyjohns, Rogers and Jacksons; and a selection of original poems entitled *After All That We've Been Through* (2023).

R.O. is married to the former Judy Grizzle of Dahlonega, Georgia. The couple make their home in Roswell and Rockmart, Georgia. Olin also has a son – Burke – by a former marriage. He and his talented wife, Olga, have produced two wonderful grandchildren – Alexander and Catherine.

# Index

www.ingramcontent.com/pod-product-compliance
Lightning Source LLC
Chambersburg PA
CBHW060543130626
46553CB00002B/879